W9-BMI-991

SAFE
ROAD
HOME

SAFE
ROAD
HOME

STOP YOUR TEEN FROM
DRINKING & DRIVING

KAREN GOODMAN & KIRK SIMON

STERLING PUBLISHING
NEW YORK

Published by Sterling Publishing Co., Inc.
387 Park Avenue South, New York, NY 10016

Distributed in Canada by Sterling Publishing
c/o Canadian Manda Group, 165 Dufferin Street
Toronto, Ontario M6K 3H6

Distributed in Great Britain by Chrysalis Books
64 Brewery Road, London N7 9NT, England

Distributed in Australia by Capricorn Link (Australia) Pty. Ltd.
P.O. Box 704, Windsor, NSW 2756, Australia

ISBN 1-4027-3278-3

Library of Congress Cataloging-in-Publication Data

Goodman, Karen. Simon, Kirk
Safe road home : stop your teen from drinking and driving / Karen Goodman and Kirk Simon. p. cm.
Accompanied by a DVD of an HBO documentary entitled: Smashed—toxic tales of teens and alcohol.
Includes index.
ISBN 1-4027-3278-3
1. Drinking and traffic accidents—United States. 2. Drunk driving—United States.
3. Teenagers—Alcohol use—United States. I. Simon, Kirk. II. Smashed—toxic tales of teens and alcohol. III. Title.

HE5620.D72G66 2005
363.12'57—dc22
2005022794

1 3 5 7 9 10 8 6 4 2

Jacket and interior design by 3+Co., New York

Printed and bound in the United States of America
DVD manufactured in the United States of America

**For information about custom editions, special sales, premium and
corporate purchases, please contact Sterling Special Sales Department
at 800-805-5489 or specialsales@sterlingpub.com.**

CONTENTS

For our children

Oliver & Allegra

and

everyone's children

INTRODUCTION
CHALLENGING THE INVINCIBLE ME

It would be comforting if we could say this book is about aberrant, fringe teen behavior. It isn't. It's about ordinary kids: your kids, our kids, anybody's kids. And, equally scary, it's about the kids who are loose cannons; kids that may literally cross paths with those we love. Kids who enter our lives through a late-night telephone call that includes nightmare words like "wreck" and "emergency room" ... It's about the needless, pointless devastation and tragedy caused by underage drinking and driving. The problem is so omnipresent that we're tempted to spell it as one word, *drinkinganddriving.*

Year after year, the statistics lay it out for us in hard, cold numbers: Motor vehicle crashes are the leading cause of injury and death for 15- to 20-year-olds. Not just a contributor. Not just one cause among many. The leading cause. And nearly half of these crashes involve alcohol. The term "accident" just doesn't apply. These alcohol-driven crashes are preventable.

Regardless of your individual family values or views concerning alcohol, the goal to focus on is getting your child home safe. No other intervention has such significant life-saving potential. Believe it or not, about three out of every ten Americans will be involved in an alcohol-related "accident" at some time in their lives. That makes "it can never happen to me" one of the most dangerous myths ever—and one of the most prevailing considering that teens have a truly awesome certainty concerning their own individual invincibility.

David Elkind, Ph.D., a noted expert on child development at Tufts University in Boston, writes that "they have what I call the personal fable, which is the belief that they are different, special. 'Other people will grow old and die. But not me!' ... That's how kids can get into trouble—because they think they're special." Elkind describes this as "a story that young adolescents tell themselves ... with themselves as protagonist. This fable makes one feel omnipotent and indestructible; immune to consequences."

In other words, bulletproof.

It's a no-brainer that thinking you're invincible encourages risky behavior.

Teens are especially good at this. What they are not so good at, sadly, is recognizing how especially vulnerable their developing bodies and brains are to the perils of drinking and driving. This book will show how and why those two Ds just don't mix—except as a lethal combination. Even when alcohol is not the primary cause of disaster, it's a principal contributor. For instance: When they're drinking, drivers of any age are less likely to use seatbelts. In 2002, more than three-quarters of the young drivers who had been drinking before they were killed were not wearing seatbelts. And that's a typical year.

Harvard educator and physician John Knight calls this image of personal immortality "a developmental phenomenon during adolescence," and it's an ailment that only time and experience can cure. "All the militaries of the world have taken advantage of this blind faith for years and years. It's not just because 18-year-olds are more physically fit that they're sent into the front lines. It's also because they tend to be fearless. Many keep believing they'll live forever until it's too late to believe anything."

At just about the age they are learning to drive, mid-adolescence, these fragile creatures are at the pinnacle of the transformation between thinking only about what's going on right now and more abstract reasoning—which would include the ability to plan ahead: What am I going to do if I get into a difficult situation?

Teens tend to live in the moment. Part child and part adult, they are searching for identity and bearing the delusions of grandeur that can accompany that search. Their attitude—which can be both admirable and deathly dangerous—is "I can take on the world!" What's missing is foresight; you're not likely to work at developing survival skills if you don't think you'll need them. Noted educator Janet Stork—consultant to the Harvard-affiliated education think tank called Project Zero—quite seriously compares teen behavior to that of toddlers: Both are struggling through extreme states of development. She likens the need to say "no" during "the terrible twos" to the teen's overwhelming desire to exert independence and power: "Some equate the ability to drink with a symbol of adulthood—now they have access to the forbidden fruit. And all too often they don't comprehend the more subtle impact of alcohol. They really believe that if they're not completely plastered they won't get hurt."

Yes, we have laws about alcohol consumption. No, they don't solve the problem. Though the severity of a crash increases with alcohol involvement, your life may depend on simply understanding that drinking a lot less than the law allows can still impair your driving. Most states set the legal limit of blood alcohol between .08 and .10. Yet driving skills start falling apart at much lower levels. The ability to steer a car while responding to changes in traffic deteriorates with a blood alcohol level as low as .02. That's one-quarter of the legal figure. Combine that with inexperience and the particularly vulnerable aspects of the teen brain, and you've got a roadmap to disaster. (Here's another grimly ironic thought: Drivers under the age of 18 are likely to have below-average driving skills and above-average alcohol consumption.)

The essential goal of this book is to create an uncomplicated and unequivocal awareness that alcohol and motor vehicles are a deadly combo—especially for underage drivers. This explosive mix can turn an ordinary automobile into a weapon of destruction. No matter what your teen's or your own attitude toward alcohol is, this is a harsh reality that just cannot be rationalized away.

It's absolutely true that substances other than alcohol can seriously impair driving, but that doesn't soften the fact that drinking and driving remains a leading cause of teenage death in America. This isn't a new problem—we've all known and tried to ignore it for years—which makes it even more tragic. And it's not just the drunk drivers who are in peril. Hundreds of thousands of passengers of all ages have their lives devastated every year by someone else's drinking and driving.

Safe Road Home offers both food for thought and practical suggestions from experts for bringing this issue to the forefront of teen and parental awareness. We talked to teens across the country about their experiences and suggestions to make this a realistic and viable tool. Overall, the key to prevention seems to be communication between parents and kids. "Young adolescents are often nervous and confused as they face their first opportunity to try alcohol: kids in this age group may be most open to your thoughts on the subject," writes Shelley Greenfield in a Harvard Medical School Special Report.

Talk with your teen to create an agreed-upon plan should they find themselves in a potentially dangerous situation. Teens who don't have a comfortable plan to count on may actually fear parental wrath more than they fear for their own personal safety—putting themselves and others at risk instead of phoning home for help.

This book offers ways to begin those life-saving conversations that can lead your kids onto that *Safe Road Home.*

CHAPTER 1

WHAT YOU DON'T KNOW CAN HURT YOU

QUIZZES ON DRINKING & DRIVING FOR TEENS & PARENTS

1 | WHAT YOU DON'T KNOW CAN HURT YOU:
QUIZZES ON DRINKING & DRIVING FOR TEENS & PARENTS

DRINKING AND DRIVING. RIDING WITH A DRIVER WHO'S BEEN drinking. You know both are bad ideas, but whether you're a teen or the parent of one, there are probably some things that you don't know about alcohol and driving—things that could make the difference between a fatal accident and getting home safely. And that's why we've created these quizzes—one for teens, one for parents. It's our hope that by creating a way to challenge your knowledge about this deadly topic, both age groups may learn some eye-opening facts about drinking and driving.

Chances are everyone in the family is going to find some surprising facts here—some scary, some shocking, and almost certainly some that you've wondered about. When you are all finished, sit down and talk to each other about those facts—all of them.

TEEN QUIZ : QUESTIONS

1. **What is the legal drinking age?**
   a. 16
   b. 19
   c. 20
   d. 21

2. **What percentage of 16-year olds have had experience with alcohol?**
   a. 20%
   b. 35%
   c. 55%
   d. 70%

3. **How many drinks would it take to make an average-size teenage boy drunk?**

4. **How many drinks would it take to make an average-size teenage girl drunk?**

5. **Is it safe to drive with a teen driver who has had one drink? Three drinks? Five drinks?**

6. **On a typical weekend in the United States, how often do you think a teen dies in a car crash?**
   a. Every 30 minutes
   b. Every hour
   c. Every two hours
   d. Every 24 hours

7. **In the United States, roughly how many teens die in alcohol-related car crashes each year?**
   a. 750
   b. 1,250
   c. 1,750
   d. 2,250
   e. 5,000

8. **Are more boys or girls involved in alcohol-related car crashes?**

9. **When do most teen car crashes occur?**
   a. During the week
   b. Over the weekend

10. **What time of day do most teen car crashes occur?**
    a. 9:00 p.m. to 2:00 a.m.
    b. 4:00 a.m. to 11:00 a.m.
    c. Noon to 9:00 p.m.

11. **Are accidents more likely to occur when a teen is driving alone or with friends in the car?**

12. **In general, how do you think teens measure up against older drivers?**
    a. More safe
    b. As safe
    c. Less safe

13. **If you were drinking and driving and were stopped by police, what do you think would happen?**

14. **When teens are involved in severe car crashes are they more likely to live or die?**

15. **For those who live, what are the most common injuries?**

16. **If you were at a party and one of your friends had been drinking, would you**
    a. Accept a ride home from them
    b. Avoid them
    c. Encourage them not to drive

17. **Do you think any of your friends could be involved in an alcohol-related car crash?**

18. **Do you think you could be involved in an alcohol-related car crash?**

TEEN QUIZ : ANSWERS

1. **d >** *The legal drinking age for every state in the United States is 21 years old.*

2. **d >** *It isn't legal anywhere, but the Centers for Disease Control and Prevention (CDC) reports that 70% of 16-year-olds have consumed alcohol. This means that the teen driving you home has probably had experience with alcohol even if you haven't. Whether you're a driver or passenger, if alcohol is involved, your car will stop being a simple transportation method and become a potential weapon of destruction.*

3. *On average, girls weigh less than boys. Thus, a 100-pound girl needs just*
4. *two drinks to be considered legally drunk—while a 150-pound boy needs two-and-a-half drinks. One drink equals a 12-ounce beer, five ounces of wine, or one shot of liquor.*

5. *Trick question. Obviously, you know that getting into a car with someone who has had five drinks is like volunteering to commit suicide. There is no point in debating degrees of suicide—when it comes to driving a car, any amount of alcohol is unsafe. Nonetheless, The Journal of Adolescent Health reported this alarming stat: within any given month, one-third of teens have driven with someone who has consumed some amount of alcohol.*

6. **b >** *On a typical weekend in the United States, one teen dies in an auto accident every hour. That means 48 will die next weekend.*

7. **e >** *Each year about 5,000 teens receive a self-invoked death penalty from drinking and driving. The National Highway Traffic Safety Administration (NHTSA) puts it simply: car crashes are the number one cause of death for individuals ages 16 to 20 years old. Furthermore, alcohol is involved in nearly half of these crashes.*

8. *Even though boys typically need to drink slightly more alcohol than girls to get drunk, they are also twice as likely as teen girls to drive drunk, according to a recent report from the National Institutes of Health (NIH). Furthermore, teen boys get into twice as many car crashes involving alcohol than teen girls.*

9. **b** > *There is a 50% greater risk for a car crash over the weekend than during the week. Though there have been no studies pinpointing why, weekend drinking is probably the culprit.*

10. **a** > *Night driving represents so great a danger that many states using graduated drivers licenses either restrict teen driving to daytime or require a teen to drive with an adult during evening hours. According to the Insurance Institute for Highway Safety, 27% of driving deaths among 16- to 19-year-olds occur between 9:00 p.m. and 2:00 a.m. The hour that represents the biggest danger for teens is Saturday night from midnight to 1:00 a.m.*

    However, it's still important to point out that the greatest number of teen crashes occur during the exact times that teens are most likely to drive. So, while Saturday night presents the biggest danger for a teen driver, the second biggest time period for crashes is Sunday afternoon. Teens also drive more during the summer, when school is out, and the Progressive Group of Insurance Companies reports that the highest teen fatalities occur in June, July, and August.

11. *Though the old proverb says, "there's safety in numbers"—and parents often prefer their kids to travel with friends—the NIH reports that with every additional teen passenger in the car, the risk grows greater. That's because if one friend can distract you, more can really distract you, making it harder to concentrate on the road and the wheel.*

12. **c** > *The NHTSA reports that with or without alcohol on board, teens are four times more likely than older drivers to get into a crash. Teens are simply less experienced drivers, and less experience means that anything impairing your ability to focus on the road—like alcohol—adds to the likelihood of an accident.*

13. *There are severe penalties for underage drinking and driving. To start, you'll lose your license. You can also go to jail.*

TEEN QUIZ : ANSWERS

14. *Live—but not happily ever after. You can suffer moderate to severe physical or mental handicaps. We've met scores of teens who survived crashes, but who must now live with devastating chronic injuries, leaving them wheelchair-bound, disfigured, or brain damaged. And let's not forget those who live every day with the horrible guilt of knowing that their drunk driving killed someone else—they won't forget, ever.*

15. *Facial disfigurement and brain damage from head injuries, spinal damage that includes permanent paralysis, injuries to important internal organs, and broken limbs are all agonizingly common in these crashes. In other words, the events of one night (often in a few seconds of that night) can determine not only if you'll live, but how you'll live—and look—for the rest of your life.*

16. **c >** *It should be no surprise that encouraging a friend not to drive is the best choice. We'll talk later about strategies you can use to help save lives—maybe your own.*

17. *The sad reality here is yes, and yes. Even though you may never drink and*
18. *drive, you can easily find yourself a passenger of someone who does—and you may not even know it. But if you're smart, you can tilt the odds in your favor, protecting yourself and your friends.*

PARENT QUIZ : QUESTIONS

1. **At what age does the average young person first try alcohol?**
   a. 10   b. 12   c. 15   d. 16   e. 17   f. 18

2. **Where are teens most likely to drink?**
   a. At home   b. At a friend's house
   c. In their own or someone else's car   d. In bars   e. Outdoors

3. **When teens consume alcohol, how do they most often obtain it?**
   a. Using fake IDs at a supermarket
   b. Using fake IDs at a liquor store
   c. Taking it from their parents or friends' parents
   d. Getting it from older siblings who purchase it legally

4. **What is the percentage of teen car crashes that involve alcohol?**
   a. 25%   b. 50%   c. 75%   d. 100%

5. **What percentage of parents say they have spoken to their teens in the past month about drinking and driving?**
   a. 25%   b. 50%   c. 75%   d. 100%

6. **What percentage of teens say their parents have spoken to them in the past month about drinking and driving?**
   a. 25%   b. 50%   c. 75%   d. 100%

7. **Does a parent's alcohol consumption influence a teen's relationship with alcohol?**

8. **If your teen called you from a party at 1:00 a.m. asking for a ride home, would you:**
   a. Be relieved he or she called to ask   b. Be annoyed
   c. Reprimand, or even punish, him or her for calling
   d. Be happy, especially since you actively—and regularly—encourage him or her to call you any time of day or night for a safe ride

9. **In the scenario above, which answer would your teen guess you'd select?**

PARENT QUIZ : ANSWERS

1. **b >** *The American Medical Association (AMA) reports that the average young person tries alcohol for the first time at the ripe old age of 12. It's clear that kids can access alcohol at a surprisingly young age.*

2. **a & b >** *According to a study by the Century Council, a Washington, D.C.– based industry organization created to promote responsible alcohol use, teens do most of their drinking in their own homes or in those of friends. In most teen peer groups, on any given weekend evening, it's likely that someone's parents won't be home.*
   (It's important to note that while answer c. [in their own or someone else's car] is not the correct answer to this particular question, drinking in a vehicle isn't uncommon. Not only do bars ask for an ID, local police have extensive knowledge of outdoor teen hangouts. Thus, teens often resort to a place that is easily accessed: a car. Unfortunately, a car is generally the most deadly place to drink.)

3. **c >** *Teens' primary sources of alcohol are their parents' cabinets or their friends' parents' cupboards. In fact, the Century Council report states that 52% of alcohol consumed by teens is obtained from parents' cabinets. Teens are often drinking YOUR ALCOHOL AT HOME! Disconcerting as this is, the good news is that this type of underage drinking is easily controlled: simply don't allow teens in your home unattended, and be scrupulous about checking whether parents will be at the homes your teen is visiting.*
   (A note about answers a and b: not long ago, a 19-year-old college student we interviewed proudly demonstrated—in exacting detail—how to fake an ID. With some computer know-how, a little ingenuity, a decent scanner/printer, and a laminating machine, a fake identity card is not difficult to create. Even if your teen doesn't own a scanner or laminating machine, these tools are readily available at schools, friends' homes, and local copy shops. Furthermore, in many communities there are thriving black markets for fake IDs.)

4. *Alcohol is involved in about 50% of fatal teen car crashes. The National Highway Traffic Safety Administration (NHTSA) reports that 29% of teen driver traffic-related deaths involve an intoxicated driver; factoring in their passengers raises the death toll to 50%.*

Notice that we refer to these incidents as "crashes" rather than "accidents." The word "accident" implies that nothing could be done to prevent the incident—which you'll soon see is not the case.

5. **c >** *According to the Century Council survey mentioned at left, 75% of parents reported speaking to their teen in the past month about the dangers of drinking and driving.*

6. **a >** *On the other hand, only 25% of teens reported having such a conversation. There's nothing new about teens not listening to their parents. When it comes to drinking and driving, however, it pays to repeat yourself as many times as necessary. The goal of this book is to stimulate these conversations about drinking and driving, and to help make them heard and understood.*

7. *Of course! A parent's behavior greatly influences his or her kid's behavior. When it comes to drinking, the "do as I say not as I do" parental approach can have tragic consequences.*

8. **d >** *The answers to these two questions are critical; d. is clearly the best*
9. *option. During the making of the documentary* Smashed: Toxic Tales of Teens and Alcohol, *we spent hundreds of hours in the Emergency Room and Trauma Unit of Maryland's Shock Trauma Hospital. Time and time again we saw teens brought in who knew they'd had too much to drink, knew they were in a potentially dangerous, life-threatening situation, but— and this is a big but—were too afraid to call their parents. Conversely, many parents said they assumed their teenager knew that "of course we would have gotten out of bed at any hour to pick him or her up." Unfortunately, this deadly communication gap is too common. It can also be fatal. Addressing this barrier is the first step in getting teens home safe.*

ALCOHOL ONBOARD

Exactly what happens when alcohol is consumed? Where does it go, and how long before its effects on the body are felt? You may be surprised by the biological journey of an alcoholic beverage, aka a "drink."

As you sip, the stomach absorbs 20% of a drink's alcohol content, while 80% is absorbed in the small intestine. Then, it heads straight for the bloodstream. How fast this happens depends on the amount of food in your stomach and the strength (read: alcohol percentage) of the drink consumed. Food in the stomach slows down alcohol's journey into the bloodstream. Drinks with higher concentrations—or proofs—of alcohol enter the bloodstream more quickly than those with lower proofs, so a sip of straight vodka will have a greater effect than the same-size sip of beer, for instance.

Once alcohol enters your bloodstream it can be easily measured by what is known as Blood Alcohol Content or BAC. In a healthy person, blood circulates all around the body—from the heart to the lungs to your brain and other organs—in about 90 seconds. This means that once alcohol enters your bloodstream you will notice the effects of that sip within 90 seconds. Your brain—being your body's most important organ—demands a sizable portion of your blood supply. As a result, alcohol has a direct path to, and quick effect upon, the brain.

It takes somewhere between 30 and 45 minutes before alcohol can actually be measured in your bloodstream. After your first drink, your BAC level will be about .02 or even higher. You may feel a little more relaxed and your body a little warmer. If you have a second or third drink over a short period of time, your reaction time will become slowed and your BAC will be around .05. By your fourth or fifth drink, your speech may become slurred, your coordination lessened, and your thinking slowed. Your BAC will be about .08 and you will be legally drunk. (Note: People who are particularly sensitive to alcohol may feel drunk consuming far fewer than four or five drinks.)

In general, alcohol tends to affect women more quickly and more intensely than men. First, a woman's body contains less water than a man's (52% versus 61%), meaning a man's body dilutes alcohol (thus minimizing its effects) more than a woman's body—even if the woman and man in question are the same weight. But because most men are larger than most women, male bodies contain even more water, which works to further dilute alcohol. In fact, every 10 pounds of body weight slightly decreases the effect of alcohol on the body and the brain. So, if the average teen girl weighs about 125 pounds and the average teen boy weighs about 165, she would become legally drunk after her third drink, while it would take four drinks for him to reach the same BAC level. Second, women's livers contain less of the enzyme needed to break down alcohol, meaning drinks are processed more slowly by a female's liver than by a male's.

How, then, does your body get rid of alcohol? The body wisely recognizes alcohol as something harmful and immediately begins a process of expelling it. Five percent of the alcohol you consume will be eliminated through sweat and urine. Your breath will eliminate another 5% through aspiration. It's common knowledge that some alcohol is expelled through the mouth during the Breathalyzer test. This test simply measures the alcohol on your breath in order to calculate how much alcohol is in your bloodstream.

Your liver does the bulk of the clean-up, as that's where 90% of the alcohol is processed. The liver is a marvelous organ, but it can only cleanse about one drink an hour. If you consume more than one drink an hour, the alcohol from that drink winds up in your bloodstream. Nothing can speed your liver's ability to process the alcohol. Coffee can't speed up the process—it will only create a slightly more awake drunk. A shower can't affect the process—it will only create a cleaner, or perhaps better-smelling, drunk. The only thing that can influence the process is time.

The Rolling Stones have it right when they sing, "Time is on My Side." If you have three drinks, for instance, your body needs three hours to process and eliminate those drinks.

When it comes to driving, alcohol in any amount—starting with just one drink—can have deadly effects. So, if you drink, and driving a car is in your near future, it becomes vitally important to have a strategy. Many options are available; you'll make a better choice if you think out the situation before you begin drinking. It doesn't matter what "exit strategy" you choose—as long as it's a safe one. We offer a number of them throughout this book.

WHAT IS A DRINK, ANYWAY?

In order to gauge how much alcohol you've consumed, it's important to know what exactly is referred to by a "drink." A "drink" is defined as any beverage that contains 0.6 ounces of pure alcohol. The most common alcoholic beverage servings all contain the same amount of alcohol: 12 ounces of 5% beer, 5 ounces of 12% wine, or 1½ ounces of 40% (80-proof) liquor such as vodka, scotch, or bourbon. It's not unlike Gertrude Stein's poetic observation that "a rose is a rose is a rose": Whether you're having a mug of beer, a glass of wine, or a shot of hard liquor, they all contain the same amount of alcohol.

Dr. Aaron White, an alcohol researcher at Duke University Medical School, was curious about how much college students actually knew about standard drink sizes. So he conducted a study with more than 100 college kids. "Students haven't been taught how to define standard drinks accurately," he found. "They tend to not understand the appropriate size, leading them to over-pour drinks and under-report levels of consumption."

It's easy to tally the number of beers consumed: just count the empty 12-ounce cans. If you've had three 20-ounce containers, you know you've had more than three drinks—i.e., 60 ounces of beer divided by the standard 12-ounce serving means five drinks.

Some drinks are deceiving: A standard glass of wine is usually listed at 5 ounces. Most wine glasses can hold 10 or 12 ounces. So 5 ounces isn't even half full. A wine glass filled 75% must be counted as 1½ servings of alcohol. Bartenders often fill glasses to that 75% point.

Inconsistency is especially prevalent in hard-liquor portions. If you take a tall glass, put in a couple of ice cubes, fill it with 7–8 ounces of vodka, then top it off with a splash of OJ, you are holding a drink that contains 5 servings of alcohol. That makes you a binge drinker ("binge drinking" means having four drinks within an hour for females and five drinks within an hour for males). So actually that "one drink" would render you legally drunk by the time you finished it.

Dr. White found that once students were clearly shown what constituted a drink they were more accurate in self-assessing their own intake. Knowing precisely how much alcohol is in every drink you take is critical. It really comes down to arithmetic—alcohol arithmetic—in which an apparently "safe" one plus one can add up to a lethal four or five.

LIFE—SAVING LANGUAGE

ADVICE FROM DR. JOHN KNIGHT ABOUT TALKING TO TEENS

2

LIFE-SAVING LANGUAGE:
ADVICE FROM DR. JOHN KNIGHT
ABOUT TALKING TO TEENS

JOHN KNIGHT, M.D., IS WIDELY RECOGNIZED AS ONE OF THE
nation's leading voices on the subject of teens and alcohol.
A physician and educator, he is the founder and director of the Center
for Adolescent Substance Abuse Research (CeASAR) at Children's
Hospital Boston. He is also associate director for Medical Education
at the Division on Addictions at Harvard Medical School, where he is
an associate professor of Pediatrics.

Dr. Knight has led numerous national studies on adolescents and
substance abuse, and he has served as a consultant to the National
Institute on Alcohol Abuse and Alcoholism, the National Institute on
Drug Abuse, and the President's Office of National Drug Control Policy.

Father of a college-age son and pre-teen daughter, Dr. Knight
has not only professional but personal experience in talking to kids
about difficult issues—practicing what he preaches. We asked him
about some of the often-intimidating problems parents face when
approaching the critical subject of teenage drinking and driving.

Q. At what age is it appropriate to begin talking to kids about the dangers of drinking and driving?

A. *I think you should start talking with your kids about alcohol and drugs around age nine. In fact, in Massachusetts we just produced a public service announcement asking parents to start having that conversation with their pre-teenaged children. But it's in a developmentally appropriate fashion; nine-year-olds obviously aren't going to be driving for a while. So I think the conversations you have with pre-teen kids are, "Do you know what alcohol is? Do you know what it does to your body? Do you know what it means to get drunk?"*

I always suggest that parents seek moments of opportunity, which come up when you're watching television and there's a story of a crash or some other tragedy related to alcohol. Or it's in the newspaper. You start calling it to your kids' attention. "Did you see this story? What a tragic thing that happened to these beautiful young people. Isn't that awful?" And that needs to start happening during the pre-teen years.

The more serious discussions about drinking and driving obviously would happen about the time that the child would go for his/her driving license. But years before that, you have to have conversations with your kids about not getting into a car with an intoxicated driver. Because you don't have to have a driver's license to get killed in an alcohol-related car crash. If you look at national survey data (from the National Youth Risk Behavior Surveillance) it's about 30% of kids who report getting into a car with an intoxicated driver within the past month. If you think about that, that's really alarming.

Q. Kids see their families and others go out to dinner, have a beer, some wine, or a cocktail and then drive home. How do you explain what might seem like a double standard to your kids?

A. *It's what other people are doing. Parents should just make a statement that that's very risky and it's wrong. I think what parents should do when they go out is, whichever parent is driving should make a point of either not having alcohol or having no more than one drink and announcing it in front of the kids. "I can only have one or I'm not going to drink because I'm the driver tonight." Because if you do that, if you model that as a family exercise, that's more powerful than any conversation you can ever have with your kids later.*

The most important thing, in my opinion, that parents have to do is model wholesome or responsible behavior. Because if the parents aren't modeling good behavior, then communication will just fall flat. So I would start with that. Parents are of legal age so they're entitled to drink. But I think parents have to drink responsibly. Their children should not see them drunk and their children should never see them getting into the driver's seat if they've had more than one drink.

In my family, I will not have a drink and drive the car. I just won't do it. So my kids have never seen that. I believe it myself; it gives my kids a very, very important message. But I think it's a harsh line to take. Would it be terrible if a parent who's going to drive had one drink? No. I don't think that's a terrible message. You're drinking responsibly. But I think once you go over that—to two or three drinks—now you're getting yourself up close to the legal limit. And that's a really dangerous message to send to kids.

The preferred thing would be for the parent who was driving to just say, "I'm not going to drink." It's just a great message to give to kids. But if parents think that's too harsh, then I would say stop at one. Don't have more than one—don't even put yourself close. Kids are such keen observers. They'll see this and they'll note it. And they won't say anything to the parents. But when I interview kids, they can tell me the exact number of drinks that their parent had before driving a car.

My own kids—they live to see me make mistakes. There is nothing that they love more than seeing me mess up on something. So, since I know that, it gives me great incentive to try to model for them appropriate behavior.

Q. What can you tell teens about the dangers of drinking and driving that they might not know, but might find convincing?

A. A common rationalization I hear from kids is "Well, I can hold my liquor. I'm a good driver. You know, somehow I'm different. Not a problem for me." I try to tell kids about some of the science. That in fact, because of their age, their brain responds differently to alcohol. It has a different effect on the teenage brain than it does on the adult brain. There's scientific evidence that shows that alcohol has less of a somnolent effect on the teenage brain—and a relatively greater effect on impairing visual-spatial perception. This is a very dangerous combination. So teenagers can drink more and stay awake, yet their ability to drive is more impaired. In some ways, if you pass out after a few drinks, it's protective because then you can't get into the car and drive. In other words, teenagers tend to be more wide awake but more impaired drunks than adults. So they're at much greater risk.

I'm in favor of anything that works. And I think that fear can work, but it's very short-lived. It has an immediate effect but it doesn't persist over time. And that may be true of a lot of interventions, which is one of the reasons it's important for parents to communicate frequently with their kids about this. The difficulty is that when you're talking to kids before they have had the experience of being injured, they believe they are invulnerable. So it's a real hard sell.

In intervention work with kids in our research studies, some of the things that we point out about alcohol are the costs—what you could be doing with the money if you didn't spend it on alcohol. We do the same with drugs, of course. And calories with alcohol—it's sometimes very helpful, especially with the girls, to point out the number of calories and what that would translate into in terms of slices of pizza. We actually do have a graphic where we show them this is how much you're drinking over the period of a month. This is how many slices of pizza that would equal, and the calories. It's a powerful image to give to them. Overall, I don't think it's so much the "magic words." I don't think parents have to worry, "Am I going to say exactly the right thing?" Kids understand what your concerns are when you bring the topic up. A lot of it is asking them what their thoughts and feelings are, asking them what's going on with their friends, trying to be a good listener, and just expressing your concern and your expectations. The big thing is just looking for the opportunities. Because they come up all the time.

Q. When is it most effective to have these talks?

A. *I urge parents to take advantage of every opportunity in the media—if there's something on television or in the newspaper. And unfortunately, there are all too many stories about this in the media.*

While the weather at this time of the year (late spring and early summer) up here in New England is beautiful, it's also my least favorite time because of the number of alcohol-related tragedies that are associated with proms and graduation. I know that every year young people in my community are going to get killed and maimed because of alcohol-related accidents. So whenever there's a story like that, there's an opportunity to talk about it. And whenever the kids are planning to go out to some kind of peer event, it's another opportunity to go over what the expectations are. We went through this with my son, who's now 22. I would use captive moments. Car rides are good, because they can't get out of the car. And it's not like the TV is on and distracting them. You have their attention while you're in the car. The other thing I always did with my son is I talked to him on the ski lift because I knew I had about six minutes and his only alternative was to jump. And after a while, it became sort of a comic thing between us. Whenever I would take him skiing we'd get on the lift and he would turn to me and say, "Okay Dad, go ahead and start the quiz. Let's just get it over with."

Q. Ideally, how often should the subject be addressed?

A. The mistake I see a lot of parents make is that they think, "I had this conversation once and that was enough." Parents have to have frequent conversations about this. My rule of thumb is that until your kids start complaining—"Oh no! Not that talk again"—you're just not doing it enough. It has to come up repeatedly—maybe once a month. And it has to be consistent. That's the key.

There was a study a number of years ago that actually showed that there was reduced drinking when parents had the conversation frequently. It's really consistency. I can't think of anything where I had just one conversation with my son and it sunk in. It was the things that I just came back to again and again and again. That's how you give them the message that it's important.

Q. Are there times you'd recommend not having the discussion?

A. If your kid comes home intoxicated, I don't think there's any point in having a discussion that evening. I think what you do is make sure they're safe, you know, get them to bed. Make sure they're rolled up on their side and talk to them the next day.

You need to have a calm discussion about what you're going to do. I don't think your kids hear anything when you're yelling and when you're speaking to them out of anger. That's a hard thing for a parent but you have to cool off and have the discussion again when you're calmed down.

GIRLS, WHAT TO DO IF...

"We often hear from young girls who tell us they're terrified by their boyfriend's drinking and driving. And they don't know how to get out of that situation," says Dr. Knight. "What we suggest to them is that they say 'I think I'm going to throw up!' Because that's the one thing that'll get the boyfriend to stop the car. If you say to a boy, 'Pull over, I don't want you to drive,' that'll go nowhere. But if your boyfriend thinks you're going to throw up in his car, he'll always stop. Then, you should call a parent or other trusted adult on a cell phone or nearby payphone."

Q. How can parents encourage their child to actually take them up on providing a safe ride home rather than risk drinking and driving or being a passenger of someone who's been drinking?

A. *If I knew that, I'd probably be in Washington. That's the frustrating part— I don't know how you can force it. I think kids have a lot of trouble taking advantage of that parental offer.*

How can we get more kids to call their parents in that situation? It's an issue that's of great concern to me. I don't know the answer. One thing that I would suggest—although this is an untested approach but a promising idea—is that when parents have that conversation, they should almost try to role-play it out.

"What would it be like for you to call me?" I don't think it's realistic to think your kid's going to be at a party at a friend's house where everyone's drinking and having a jolly time and they're going to pull their cell phone out all of a sudden and say, "Mommy, please come pick me up. I don't think I can get home safe." So it might be, let's have some kind of a family code word, so if you call and say to me, "Did Melissa leave a message for me?" That means, "I need you to give me a ride home," or "I'm worried about my ride home."

You really have to get into the details. I did that with my son. And he never called me, but to my knowledge, he also never came home with an intoxicated driver. You have to get to the specifics of how this would actually happen rather than just talking about it as a theoretical idea.

I was just on a panel with one of the district attorneys from Middlesex County in Massachusetts. She talked about a survey they did on the

"Contract For Life" that SADD (Students Against Destructive Decisions; formerly Students Against Drunk Driving) puts out. *It's an agreement between parents and kids that essentially says "you can call me anytime and I'll provide safe transportation for you and I won't get in your face that night. We'll discuss it later."*

Their survey showed that 80% of parents said they would do it, yet only about 15% of kids said they would ever call their parents in that situation. And I don't know what the answer is to that. It's actually an interesting research question and we're embarking on a study now where we're going to try to explore that a little bit further to see if there's any way we can increase the numbers of young people who would be willing to call parents for safe transportation.

Q. Are there things that don't work, or that parents shouldn't do or say in these conversations?

A. *I'll tell you some of the difficult things that come up in parent communication. Parents very often will ask me, "What do I say about my own past use of alcohol?" Or it comes up with drugs as well. You know, "what do I tell my kids if they ask me, you know, did I ever do it?" And my belief is that if your kids ask you what you did when you were younger, you need to be honest. But you don't need to go into a lot of detail. And I think that you need to frame it as past mistakes. "This is what I did. I know now that it was wrong. I wish that I didn't and my hope is that you won't have to repeat my mistakes. I hope that I made some of them for you so that you don't have to do them."*

What's problematic is when parents present their own past history of drinking as like, it's funny. "Oh yes, I got so smashed and we did this and that," like it's humorous. I think that's a big mistake. And those parents need to grow up.

Q. What about kids who seem unapproachable, yet you know they're drinking and driving?

A. *My recommendation at that point would be to get professional help. I think parents need help. It's just too much for them to deal with alone. We see kids like that in our outpatient program all the time. Parents have to take some extraordinary steps. They do have to take cars away and cell phones and credit cards and access to ATMs and all sorts of other stuff. But I don't* *think parents can do that on their own. They need to get someone who's got experience in dealing with substance abuse in teenagers to help guide them through it. Sometimes the kids will refuse to go to the appointment. We tell parents to come anyway.*

Q. What would be the signs that indicate a parent should seek professional help?

A. *I have a very conservative view on this because, I'll tell you, when parents think there's a problem, there's a huge problem. Parents are usually not clued in to the early signs. And so I tell parents: when you're getting worried—if there's the first episode of where your kid is passed out or there's an emergency room visit or you know that they're using—talk to a healthcare professional at that point.*

I just don't think parents can wait. Most of them do. They don't call until it's the second or the third time. And then the typical story I hear from parents is, "Oh well, he's done this two or three times." And then we find out from the kid that they're really doing it every week, or every day. So I have a very low threshold for telling parents to seek help.

The big signposts are when your kid winds up in the emergency room or has an accident. But the more subtle signals are the changes. Changes in academic performance, changes in friends, changes in their degree of social involvement; they were on teams and in after-school activities, now they're not doing that anymore. I think parents have a sixth sense where they just feel in their stomach that something is wrong. Their kids won't talk to them anymore and they need to act when they get those signals.

Q. What about peer pressure?

A. *When it comes to alcohol and drug use, people talk about peer pressure, and I think too many parents assume that we're talking about overt peer pressure. And about your kids' friends saying to them, "Oh come on, have a drink. Oh come on, smoke a joint." That's really not what it is. It's very subtle peer pressure. It's very covert. It's just that that's what the other kids are doing and if you don't do it with them then you're really not part of the group. You don't feel like you belong. It's a very important kind of peer pressure, to feel like you won't fit in.*

Social isolation—it's very powerful. It's probably an evolutionary phenomenon, if you think about it. You know, adolescence was a very important transition time. When our ancestors were living out on the plains, if you were socially ostracized by your peers, you probably were not going to survive. Social isolation is equivalent to death for teenagers. It's huge for them.

Q. In addition to frequent talks, what other strategies would you recommend?

A. *Well, no matter what you do, you can't—unless you're going to chaperone your kid 24 hours a day—always be there. You can't absolutely prevent them from ever being exposed to alcohol. All you can do is your best: Consistent messages, modeling healthy behavior, talking with other parents; you just do your best. And then you have to hope it works out.*

Given that information, what I tell parents is that they should have a clear policy that if you're under the age of 21, the only time you're going to have a drink is with your parents. I mean, if there's a social or religious or family event and there's parental supervision, I don't think there's anything wrong. In fact, there's some evidence that allowing your child to drink with you may be protective. But what is not allowed is drinking with your peers.

There's one study that came out about a year ago that gives an odds ratio for kids who reported drinking with their parents (they're allowed to have a sip or a single drink). Their odds of binge drinking were about 1 in 3. But when parents supplied alcohol for kids to drink with their peers they doubled their risk of binge drinking.

I think kids watch their parents' consumption of alcohol. They notice how many drinks their parents are having in situations. They're aware of parent drug use at times when parents think their kids know nothing about it. And that includes both prescription drugs and illicit drugs like marijuana. It's very common for me to hear from parents, "Well, yes, I do this or that, but my kids don't know anything about it." When in fact, their kids are very aware of what's going on. Parent role-modeling is the most effective form of communication. And without modeling healthy behavior, what you say will have little or no effect.

One of the things that I try to urge parents to do is to network together in terms of the drinking and driving thing. One of the more effective strategies would be prevention, so I always tell parents they need to know where their kids are going, whose house they're going to be at. They need to make a phone call to the [friend's] parent to make sure that there's going to be a parent there and that there isn't going to be any alcohol and there aren't going to be any drugs.

I've heard back from parents who say occasionally other parents will lie about this. They'll call and then it turns out even though the parent said they were going to be around, they weren't. But that's fairly rare. I think most of the time, when you talk to another parent, you have a very good idea whether or not they're going to supervise the social gathering. Of course your kids don't really like you to do this. My son didn't like it, but he accepted it.

I'd tell my son, you can always bring your friends over to our house. Have the kids come to your house. Because if you're around and you're

PICTURES OF THE BRAIN UNDER THE INFLUENCE

Just how does a driver's brain respond to alcohol in the system? Very badly, according to a recent Yale University study.

"Imaging studies of the brain when it is under the influence of alcohol reveal that different areas of the brain are impaired under high and low levels of alcohol," the university's news release reported.

Before being seated behind the wheel for a simulated road trip—something like a deadly video game—participants in the study were given different dosages of alcohol (or a placebo). Their blood alcohol level ranged from .05 to .10. This is the equivalent of having just a little to drink or having a lot. At a level of .08, you're considered legally intoxicated—just plain drunk.

The scientists actually watched the alcohol-addled brains of drivers as they fumbled their way into simulated disaster.

Researchers were able to distinguish which areas of the brain were affected and at what blood alcohol content. The areas controlling motor functions were the most impaired. Once the legal limit was reached, decision-making areas and memory were also affected. Speeding was directly correlated with the amount of alcohol in the system, which affects the cerebellum.

The people in the test who were given the alcohol drove the way people do when they're in real cars and really intoxicated. That cerebellum-speedup, for instance, happened most especially for these drivers when going around corners—where drivers with unpolluted brains have the good sense to slow down. These drivers also crashed into other simulated vehicles more often than the mentally unimpeded drivers did.

not going to allow drinking, your house is the safest place. It's just an inconvenience. I'd do this with my son and my wife would always complain. There would be 12 kids that would come over. They'd eat everything in the refrigerator, order out pizza, they'd be loud, they'd keep us up. And I would be happy. I was just so glad that they were doing it here. And you just bear with the inconvenience because of what it means—that your kids are protected and they're safe.

Q. What excuses do parents give for not talking to their teens?

A. I believe you set a clear expectation that you're not going to go drinking with your friends until you're of legal age, until you're 21. Often when I present that to parent groups they say, "Oh, but you know that's not realistic. We know that 90% of kids are going to be drinking by the time they're seniors in high school." That's true. But as a parent, I have expectations that my kids always do their homework and that they clean their own room. Do they always meet my expectations? No. But it doesn't mean I drop the bar down and say, "Fine. You can have a messy room. Don't bother doing your homework." I still have expectations.

What I hear from parents is that they're afraid that if they don't allow their kids to drink at parties with their classmates they're going to be unpopular. That's one of the most common objections I hear. "Oh, but if I don't let my son or daughter do that then they're not going to be popular anymore." And I say to them, "Sometimes you have to give your kids the message that doing the right thing may cost you. That's part of life."

I don't think the job of the parent is to see that your kids are always happy or always popular. Because that's just not real life. Our job as parents is to prepare our kids to be responsible adults. And one of the lessons of being a responsible adult is that you need to do the right thing and sometimes you'll pay a price for doing it. But that's called "character."

I always see that parents are more interested in hearing about kids' drug use. And drug use gets a lot more attention. But from a public health perspective, alcohol is the greatest problem. It is responsible for more deaths than drug use in young people. So when I give talks to parent groups, I always start my talk with alcohol and then I'll mention drugs later on. Parents in our clinical program will come in and they'll say to me, "Dr. Knight, thank God it's only alcohol. At least they're not using drugs." Well, I wouldn't thank God too much.

TOXIC TALES FROM TRUE LIFE

THE SURVIVORS

3

TOXIC TALES FROM TRUE LIFE:
THE SURVIVORS

DEATH IS NOT THE ONLY TRAGEDY TO COME FROM DRINKING-
and-driving disasters. Those who manage to survive a crash suffer
devastating injuries; paralysis is on the top-ten list. And it's not just
bones that get broken. Traumatic brain injury is an all-too-common
result of these crashes. Simply stated, when a car crash occurs, the
vehicle may stop moving but your brain just might continue to bounce
around inside your skull. That bounce can cause severe damage,
potentially transforming a vitally alive teen into a blank-eyed toddler
in a matter of moments. This chapter offers stories of teens who
survived to tell of broken bodies, brain trauma, and shattered dreams—
the far-reaching consequences of impaired survival.

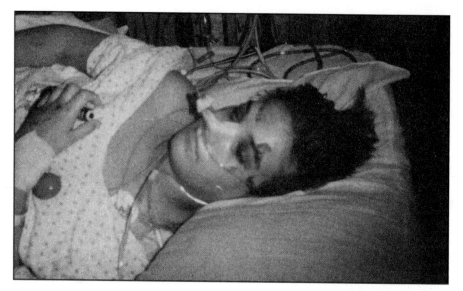
Tracy lay paralyzed for 17 hours before her broken body was rescued.

TRACY O'CONNOR

Tracy O'Connor never thought she'd end up as Ms. Wheelchair America. "I was not an angel in high school—I went to kegs, I went to parties. But I never, ever thought that this would happen to me. I thought I was invincible. But a year and three months after I graduated from high school, I was put in a wheelchair for the rest of my life."

She was 19 when it happened. She and her boyfriend Andy were on their way to do some fishing and horseback riding in the Big Horn Mountains of Wyoming at a resort owned by Andy's boss. Richard, the boss's son, was to drive them there. About three hours into the trip, around midnight, he stopped, bought a six-pack, and started drinking.

Tracy didn't know him well; he was "more or less an acquaintance." But she knew he shouldn't have been driving. "I said 'Richard, can I drive?' And he said, 'No.' I'm a girl and I was only 19 and I guess he thought I would wreck his dad's pickup. Men can be stubborn, especially when they're drinking." Tracy asked him several more times, but he still refused.

"The last thing I remember is putting my head on my boyfriend's shoulder and falling asleep," she woefully recalls. "I woke up because I felt that we were not on the road anymore. I looked out the front windshield and we were heading straight toward a fence, toward a whole bunch of trees. I looked over at the driver and his eyes were closed and I yelled, 'What are you doing?!'" Richard was asleep, his foot on the accelerator, the car speeding up to 90 mph. When Tracy woke him he panicked and jerked the wheel. The truck rolled four times. Nobody had seat belts on. On the first roll, Richard was ejected and the truck rolled on top of him, probably killing him straight away. Through the second roll, Tracy and Andy remained in the vehicle, spinning with it. On the third roll, Andy was thrown out of the car about nine feet forward onto the road. And on the vehicle's fourth roll—toward where Andy lay—the corner of an open door caught Andy in the head, piercing his skull and killing him instantly.

It was also on the truck's fourth roll that Tracy was ejected and hurled 90 feet through the air. She landed chest-first. Her legs came up over her head, bending her like an accordion. Her back broke, her spinal cord was injured. She couldn't move.

They were two football fields away from the highway, not readily visible. They weren't expected at the resort, so no one was looking for them. Barely able to move, Tracy lay on the ground the entire night. The temperature was below freezing and she struggled to put her arms underneath her body in a pitiful attempt to keep warm. The next day, falling in and out of consciousness, she lay on her stomach in the shade, unable to move into the sunshine for warmth. "I was completely paralyzed and I'd lost almost half the blood in my body through a hole in my ankle," she says. She stayed that way for 17 hours.

Finally, a couple out for a Sunday drive approached. Thinking they saw a deer, they slowed down. What they'd noticed was a stump, but because they'd slowed down they spied something else—the truck. Turning around, they discovered the accident—and the two dead bodies. "It was a miracle the way that I was found. I heard their voices and I yelled, 'I'm down here!' Thank goodness they found me when they did, because in less than an hour it was going to be dark again and there was no way I would have made it through another night. I was slowing dying out there," says Tracy.

Her mom, Karen Charlton, recalls receiving the phone call every parent dreads. "'This is doctor so-and-so, I have your daughter here and she's been in an extremely bad car accident.' I remember saying to him, 'How are the boys?' And he just never answered my question." Then, she received another call—from the coroner. "'Mrs. Charlton,'" he said, "'I want you to know that I have two dead young men here. Do you know them?'"

Tracy was taken to a tiny hospital nearby, where she had a blood transfusion before being airlifted to a larger facility in Billings, Montana. Her face was swollen to twice its normal size, ridden with cuts and scrapes, and her hair was stained with blood. When Tracy's mom first entered her hospital room, the very first thing Tracy said was, "'How are the boys?'" remembers Karen. When her mother replied that the boys didn't make it, Tracy was devastated.

Tracy's condition was too severe for the Billings hospital to deal with. In addition to her back injuries, she had a gaping hole in her left ankle so big that "when they unwrapped it my mom could literally see daylight through it. There were no tendons left, no ligaments, no muscle." They thought that a wild animal had attacked her, but it was probably something more like a tree branch piercing through her ankle. She was airlifted again, this time to Minneapolis, Minnesota, where she spent six weeks undergoing operation after operation. At the time of this writing, she's on operation number 20. They took a muscle from her stomach and skin grafts from the side of her leg to rebuild her ankle. She had fusion, rods, and screws in her back, and a reconstruction on her right knee was needed just from being thrown through the air.

Tracy went home to recover with a fixator (a bulky device fixed into the bones around a gaping wound to help soft tissues grow back over the site) in one leg and a cast on the other. Then she went to rehab to learn how to live the rest of her life in a wheelchair. She feels that she "had somebody watching over me. My life was saved that night. I'm mainly paralyzed from the knees down—unlike the two guys that were killed."

Her mom remembers the day before the wreck, when she met Tracy for lunch. "When she walked in, I thought to myself, what a neat walk Tracy has, just kind of a bounce. Her trademark is her infectious smile, and in the 19 years I've been her mother, I'd never really thought about her walk. But it has really stuck in my mind, that walk of hers. And the very next night, that was all taken away."

"You don't have to be falling-down drunk to get into a car accident," Tracy reminds us. "Richard had no more than four beers. But it was late at night, he'd been outside working all day, and he was tired. We all know beer is a depressant and I think it made him more tired and made him fall asleep at the wheel. He wasn't stumbling-down drunk but I can honestly say. . . if he wouldn't have been drinking that night, I think he still would be alive."

Today, Tracy works with a group called Think First, an organization dedicated to teaching young people how to prevent brain, neck, and spinal-cord injuries. Their motto is: Use your mind to protect the rest of your body. And she will tell anybody who will listen: "It definitely can happen and it definitely changes your life. People think when you have a spinal-cord injury, all that's affected are the obvious things, your hands and your arms and your legs. They don't think about bowels and bladders and things like that. I will spend the rest of my life in a wheelchair because of a choice the driver made, and I guess, a choice I made, too."

Brandon made a deadly decision when he got into Jesse's truck.

BRANDON WILLARD

Brandon Willard was 18. It was late July in the town of Buchanan Dam, in Texas hill country. Dana was his girlfriend. Her brother Jesse, who was Brandon's good friend, was down from the Army with his brand-new Mazda 2000 single-cab pick-up truck. The three of them went to the lake to party—it was what they did every weekend: "We'd go to the lake or to a friend's; throw little parties and stuff," said Brandon. "In the summertime, we'd swim; we camped out and we drank."

Brandon had been drinking since he was 16. He chose not to drink that night—but the others did. He and Dana had squabbled that day, and Brandon's mom, Annette, remembers that "Brandon had called me earlier. He and his girl-friend had been fighting, and he wanted me to come and get him. Something happened and he said, 'let me call you back.' He never did."

When the informal party they were at got moved elsewhere, Brandon and Jesse dropped Dana off to end the arguing. "And I thank God," Brandon says, "because she wouldn't be here today if we hadn't." Brandon and Jesse stopped at a store; Jesse was "kicked out due to his vulgar language; he was being an idiot." When they got back to the truck, Brandon—who'd still had nothing to drink—asked Jesse if he could drive. His house was just blocks from the store on a straightaway road. "Just a paved little road. You could walk there in five minutes." Even after repeated requests, Jesse refused to give up the wheel. Brandon didn't know just how intoxicated Jesse was at the time. "My last memory of that night was putting on my seat belt. Well, needless to say, we didn't go home." Instead, they went the other way. Jesse was driving at what authorities later estimated at about 110 mph, when they turned a corner in a 35-mph zone.

Swerving into the oncoming lane, they jumped the guardrail, flew about 25 feet in the air and landed 75 feet below. Lake Buchanan had dried up severely that year—so had the canal beneath the bridge, where they crashed and turned about seven somersaults before the shattered car settled down. Jesse was thrown out of the vehicle but Brandon remained in the cab through the macabre gymnastics. The seats, headrests and all, were twisted off and propelled to the back of the truck. Brandon's head went through the glass. The truck was totaled. Jesse was fine.

Brandon recalled that his martial arts instructor, Mark, a member of the volunteer fire department, lived nearby and was the first one at the scene.

Brandon's injuries rendered him a quadriplegic.

"Mark said Jesse kept slapping me in the face saying, 'Don't die on me! Don't die on me!' And they kept pushing him off."

Brandon's head was split open with a two-inch slit, through which he lost about six pints of blood. He shattered the C7, C6, and C5 vertebrae, contused the fourth vertebra, and severed his spinal cord, "which means you most likely do not live. That's like pulling the computer from the wall," Brandon declares. He couldn't be airlifted from the site because of adjacent power lines. They went by ambulance to a local hospital and Brandon was flown to Austin. Along the way, blood continued to flow from his head.

Brandon's mom was shampooing her carpets when she got the call from Dana's mom, Karen. "She asked me if I had heard about Brandon. And my first thought was, 'did he get in trouble?' She said, 'Oh my God, Annette, you have to get to the hospital! I have a friend who works there, and I just talked to her, and they're waiting for Starflight to land. Brandon has been in a very bad accident and I don't know if he's going to make it or not.'"

Annette rushed to meet the ambulance. When they opened the door, Brandon's head was all bandaged up; the bandages were "just solid red; just blood." Looking at her once-athletic, handsome son, she thought about how she'd never see him run again. She touched his face, and told him, "'Brandon I'm here, it's Mom.' I didn't know if he could hear me or not, but he opened his eyes, and the first words out of his mouth were, 'Mom, am I going to die?' And then he just closed his eyes again."

Brandon was paralyzed from the neck down. Because of the heavy pain medications, Brandon has few memories of the two-and-a-half weeks in the ICU that followed. "I remember the surgeon telling me when I was leaving the ICU that I would never move or walk again. And I told him, 'Sir, I'm going to crawl or walk out of your hospital.'" To this day, Brandon doesn't use the word "can't" when he talks about walking. Instead, he says, "I will walk one day."

Brandon spent a year in rehabilitation. For the first three months, with his neck in a brace, he still couldn't feel or move his body at all. "The humiliation that I had to go through at 18-years-old was just degrading—going to the bathroom on yourself, having people you don't know clean you up. You sit there paralyzed, you're thirsty and you have a glass of water beside you on your nightstand but you have to wait for somebody to come and give you a drink."

His girlfriend Dana was his salvation; she more or less lived with him at the hospital. "She stood by me. The nurses didn't have to do anything; she did everything for me." Brandon credits his positive attitude to her. "I never once was depressed; never once gave up."

Brandon was released in December; his relationship with Dana continued for several months. "She'll always hold a spot in my heart for what she did," he says.

Jesse was charged with assault and battery in a vehicle, alcohol-related—a charge that's just below manslaughter—but Brandon dropped the charges. The district attorney called him and said "Mr. Willard, I've been D.A. for 22 years and I've never had a victim come forth like this and drop charges."

Brandon replied: "I made the choice to get in that vehicle that night. He didn't force me. I knew what could happen. So, I have to take accountability for my own actions, just like he does, just like you do, and just like everybody else does. I made that choice and I'm paying the consequences."

In the end, Jesse got 10 years probation. He was in four subsequent crashes, all alcohol-related, including a hit-and-run. Brandon got called in when Jesse violated his probation.

"I felt like—it's going to be on my shoulders if I don't do something about it. When I took the stand, the prosecutor asked me if I believed Jesse needs 10 years of prison time. All I could say was that Jesse should be confined to a place where he's not subjected to alcohol, where it's not a temptation to him, nor is he a danger to others or himself." Jesse was finally sentenced to 10 years in prison.

Today, Brandon is a quadriplegic. He has no feeling in his hands and no finger movement. He has no triceps—when he holds his hands up in the air, they fall. Brandon's five-foot-tall mom suffers from hauling around his 200-pound wheelchair—as well as Brandon himself—to get him to and from medical appointments, sometimes four times a day. Brandon shares that suffering, too: "Sometimes I cry myself to sleep to see my mom at a young age—43, 44 years old—have to get on her knees to pick something up and then pry herself back up."

Brandon had wanted to join the Air Force since he was a kid. "And I was going to go. But that can't happen anymore. I have a little niece now, and it really hurts me because I can't pick her up and play with her and give her rides and do the stuff that I kind of want to do with my own children. I want to be able to be the father I want to be. But if I don't get use of my hands then I won't be able to change diapers, throw my kids in the air, do the Halloween thing. I won't be able to watch over a kid of my own. That hurts."

Brandon remembers speakers at his school lecturing about drinking and driving—the slide shows, the horrific graphics, and the blood. "I drank. We knew the consequences. Kids are invincible until something happens, until it's too late. Well, the day did come that it did happen to me."

Brandon's mother Annette shares her thoughts on teens drinking and driving: "Like I told Brandon and I tell the other kids, yeah we may get mad you know, it's 3:00 in the morning, you're waking us up, but I would much rather be mad at you, and tell you I love you, and be able to hug you, than not see you at all . . . Yes, it's illegal, but there's no stopping them. The most important thing that they can tell their kids is no matter what time it is—2:30, 3:00, 4:00 in the morning—and you're drinking, or your ride is drinking and they're drunk, no matter whatever, then call me and I'll pick you up, because I'd rather pick you up than come and see you in the hospital or visit you in a casket."

A tragic coincidence: Childhood pals Cortnie and Angie became victims of separate drunk-driving crashes as teens.

CORTNIE AND ANGIE

Growing up, Cortnie Stewart and Angela Moehring lived down the street from each other. During junior high school they were best friends, together every day. In high school they drifted apart, but two tragedies would align their lives forever. Two teens and two crashes, two years apart. Two similar outcomes.

CORTNIE STEWART >

Cortnie Stewart decided to take her mother's car for a drive. She was 17; she'd had her license for about a year. It was wintertime in Jonesboro, Illinois. Cortnie's family had left for Indiana on Saturday morning to see the basketball star Allen Iverson and the Philadelphia 76ers play against the Indiana Pacers; they would return on Sunday. The weather was foul, with ice and snow on the highways, and Cortnie promised her mother, Judy Stewart, that she would stay home while the family was gone.

Around 2:00 am on Sunday, Judy received the dreaded phone call: Cortnie had been in a car crash. The family left Indiana immediately, making the seven-hour trip home through a severe ice storm. The ice storm that made their journey torturously slow was also probably the reason behind the tragedy. Ignoring her own promise to stay home, Cortnie had pitted her driving skills against the elements. (Later, she would not remember where she was headed or why.) For 40 miles her self-confidence probably seemed justified. Then the car hit a patch of black ice and careened off the road. There was a culvert there, and Cortnie was flung into the shallow water of the ditch where it was 10 degrees below zero. The vehicle flipped and could have crushed her if the collision hadn't bent it into a tent-shape; Cortnie was safely held under the inverted V of the wrecked car.

Ironically, Judy thinks the ditch's far-below-freezing water is probably what saved her daughter's life. "It cools you down," she explains, "and you're in a frozen state."

Because Cortnie has no memories of her drive, many questions remain. "She didn't have her seat belt on," Judy points out in wonder. "She never went anywhere in the car without wearing her seat belt. Did she get scared and flip it off? I'll just never know."

Within 10 minutes of the crash, a state policeman found Cortnie; she was flown to nearby St. Francis Hospital in Cape Girardeau, where she lay in a coma for 13 days. When she emerged, she was yelling, crying, screaming—agonizing moments that gladdened her mother's heart nonetheless. "They told me that was good because she still had her emotions," Judy explains.

The blows to Cortnie's head, however, caused traumatic brain injuries that would forever affect Cortnie's daily activities. She "eats" through a feeding tube in her stomach. To move, she needs a person on each side of her. She doesn't have use of her left arm. She barely talks. "She knows everything," her mother says. "She's in there. They just don't know how to get her out."

ALCOHOL AND THE GENDER GAP

Men and women metabolize, absorb, and circulate alcohol differently, and a woman—alas—gets the worst of it.

A woman becomes intoxicated after drinking less than a man does. This has nothing to do with choice, emancipation, or competition. It's just biology. For one thing, women absorb more alcohol into the bloodstream than men do. The problem is water.

Pound-for-pound, a woman's body contains less water than a man's does. This means that since alcohol is water-soluble, a woman drinking the same amount will have more alcohol in her blood than a man will.

The police told Cortnie's father that they believed she had been drinking that night. If you ask Cortnie if this is so, she will nod her head. Her unspoken answer is "yes," she had been drinking. Why did Cortnie break her promise? Why did she ignore the most basic safety rules she had been taught? Judy will never know the answers, but she knows that, as a mother, she tried her best.

Cortnie's childhood friend Angie was extremely upset about Cortnie. "I went to visit her with our junior high basketball coach. She was lying there in a coma in the ICU with her eyes closed, and we just kept talking to her. I wanted to cry," says Angie. "And then it happened to me."

ANGIE MOEHRING >

At 14, Angie began drinking. She had friends who were older, and getting alcohol was never a problem for her. "I liked to act stupid," she admits, and drinking helped her to act exactly that way. She talks about drinking and driving as a casual pastime. "We went 'low-riding,' going on back roads and getting drunk," she remembers. "One time I was on a back road and I guess I was pretty drunk. I missed the corner and went through a barbed-wire fence. I was drunk probably four nights a week."

On the night that would limit her life forever, Angie was out with Gylian and Diane, two coworkers from her job at the fast-food restaurant, Hardee's. "Angie had left her car," her mom, Patricia Moehring, recalls, "which was kind of unusual because she always drove herself." The girls and two boys were on their way to a party out in the country to drink and listen to music.

Angie and Diane squabbled about who was going to sit in the front passenger seat. Unfortunately, Angie won. Diane sat in the back with the boys. Gylian took off at 85 or 90 mph to try to catch up with some friends they'd met up with earlier. "We were all telling her to slow down, but she wouldn't," Angie remembers.

The car fishtailed and then flipped. The girls in the front were ejected from the vehicle in opposite directions—Angie out the front windshield and Gylian out the back. Gylian, Diane, and the boys received only minor cuts and bruises.

Angie's mom describes the accident scene: "I don't know where the boys landed, but when the car rolled, the other girls landed on the grass," she says. "Angie got thrown several feet and she hit the pavement on her head. That's what made it so bad."

When police examined the car, it had a cooler with 16 cans of beer. Three of them were open. Gylian, who was driving, reportedly had a blood alcohol level of .04—half the legal limit.

"The first thing they told me was there was brain trauma," Patricia remembers. Angie also had a lacerated liver, broken ribs, multiple facial fractures, a broken jaw, and severe swelling in her head. She had a tracheotomy and developed six different infections that could have killed her. She was in a coma for more than a month. When she officially came out of the coma, no one knew exactly what was going to happen. "She wasn't talking or anything; she just had a glare," Patricia recalls. "We didn't know at that point if she knew us."

Cortnie's mom, Judy—who'd been through this before—tried to comfort Angie's mom. "She knew Angie was in a coma, and she would say 'Just like Cortnie.' I thought 'Oh, I just can't go through that!' It would just take me to tears. I didn't want to accept that it was the same kind of thing."

Crying, Patricia barely manages to continue the story, even now: "I guess the hardest—the worst part—came when they moved Angie out of ICU to the floor above and did a test where they put applesauce in her mouth to see if she could swallow. She couldn't. It went into her airway, and that's it. It means there's neurological damage. And that just upset me so much. When there's neuro damage, going back to anywhere close to 100% is not gonna happen."

Angie has no memory of being in the hospital. The first thing she remembers is waking up at a rehabilitation facility in St. Louis, Missouri: "I thought my mom put me in the place because I was a bad kid."

Her mother remembers the day Angie started talking. It was on the weekend before Angie's birthday that the teen first communicated. "We came around the corner and she was like, 'Hiiiiiiii. Mmmommmmmm.' It was very slow; she could just get it out. It was about three-and-a-half months after the accident."

Today, Angie walks with a limp. She can't bounce a ball, can't run. Her thinking is slowed and her reactions are delayed. "You can tell by my speech that there's something that happened to me," she says. Cognitive testing has revealed that Angie is very much a middle-schooler again. "She's this grown woman who has only the ability of a much younger person," her mom laments.

As such, Angie can't get a job. Ever since childhood, she'd wanted to be a police officer. But now that can't happen. She used to be good at the computer. But now she can only use one finger. She had a job at a hospital for a few months, but was let go because she was too slow.

A final irony in the unfortunate symmetry of Cortnie's and Angie's lives: "It's really weird," Angie's mother reflects. "They had the same attitudes and they grew up together. And then the same thing happened to Angie."

DRINKING, DRIVING & DYING: SOME SCARY STATISTICS

National Highway Traffic Safety Administration (NHTSA) reports:

- Motor vehicle crashes remain the leading cause of death and injury for 15- to 20-year-olds. Per mile, they are four times more likely to crash than anyone else. They also have the lowest rate of seat belt use.

- More Americans have died in transportation crashes than in all the wars fought in US history.

- In 2002, nearly one-third of the young drivers who were killed in motor vehicle crashes had been drinking.

- More than 75% of the young drivers killed in 2002 who were drinking were not wearing seat belts.

- As of 2002, changing the drinking law from 18 to 21 has saved about 21,887 lives since 1975.

National Youth Risk Behavior 2003 Survey, Centers for Disease Control & Prevention (CDC):

- About one-third of 12th graders reported having 5 or more drinks in a row in the previous two weeks. More than 90% said it was fairly easy or very easy to get alcohol. More than 80% of 10th graders and more than 50% of 8th graders said so too.

- More than one in three teens reported that in the last month they had ridden with a driver who had been drinking alcohol. Half of them reported having driven after drinking alcohol in that same period.

- Of the students surveyed, 27.8% had their first drink of alcohol, other than a few sips, before age 13.

Other surveys and studies:

- The University of Michigan's Monitoring the Future study (2004) reported that the proportions of 8th, 10th, and 12th graders who admitted drinking an alcoholic beverage in the 30-day period prior to the survey were 19%, 35%, and 48%, respectively. The majority of 12th graders surveyed did not view binge drinking on weekends as carrying a great risk.

- The American Journal of Preventive Medicine published a survey (May 2005) that showed driving while intoxicated is on the rise.

- The University of Chicago Medical Center reported that 30% of Americans will be involved in an alcohol-related crash in their lifetime.

CHAPTER 4

MOST TRAGIC TOXIC TALES

LIVES LOST

4 MOST TRAGIC TOXIC TALES:
LIVES LOST

NO ONE DIED IN ANY OF THE STORIES WE FOLLOWED IN THE making of our documentary, *Smashed: Toxic Tales of Teens and Alcohol.* That's statistically consistent: About 100,000 teens are involved in car crashes each year and the vast majority of those crashes don't involve fatalities. Decades ago, the percentage of teens who died in these crashes was far higher, and there are a lot of good reasons for the decrease. We have better seat belts and we have more people using them; we have anti-lock brakes; car manufacturers are making cars that better survive crashes; cell phones allow for quicker medical response and EMS systems keep improving. Still, even with all these improvements, a National Center for Statistics and Analysis report shows that 7,884 15-to-20-year-olds died in car crashes in 2003. Mechanical improvements make a difference—just not enough.

Though the stories in *Smashed* didn't end in death, during the process of making the film and researching this book, we talked to numerous other families whose stories had an even grimmer ending. There are three profiles of teens in this chapter—one was a driver, two were just passengers. All of them were "good kids from good families," and all of them were lost to the lethal combination of alcohol and driving. Their courageous families, relatives, and friends, who openly share their stories here, hope others will learn from their tragedies.

KARL KAKEDELIS

Karl Kakedelis was drinking and driving on June 27, 2003, and he was responsible for the death of one of his best buddies.

Karl appeared to be a model student. "My grades were 4.0," he recalls. "I was captain of wrestling and soccer—my high-school career shows that I did everything to be the best, that I could be perfect."

Unfortunately, this "perfect" student wasn't who the North Carolina teen truly was. "I told people what they wanted to hear," says Karl. "And I did what I wanted to do. Who I really was, was a partier; someone who was irrational, made wrong decisions, lied to get what he wanted. I lied. I told my parents I didn't drink. Well, my entire life was made up of lies, pretty much."

Wayne became a powerless passenger as he was catapulted out of his pal's car.

Karl sets the scene for the tragic night in 2003: "I was graduating from high school and I was going to continue my education at the Citadel. One of my best friends I was graduating with, Logan, said, 'Hey, do you want to throw a going-away party?' And I said, 'Sure.' I wanted to say bye to everybody. We decided to throw the party in an isolated wooded area on a lake outside of our town. We made calls to about 45 people—and 75 to 100 people showed up."

Karl was 19 years old. The day before the party, he and his friends persuaded a reluctant 21-year-old to buy a keg of beer for them. The party had to be kept a secret from their parents, so the boys hid the keg in the woods. Karl told his parents that he was going to spend the night with a friend. "The party started around midnight and we had the keg of beer," Karl explains. "We proceeded to drink and party and one of my friends called me. It was a guy I hadn't seen in a while and he said, 'Man, I heard about your party and I'm near but I can't find you.' So I tried to give him directions over the phone and he said there was so much noise and stuff going on in the background he couldn't understand. So eventually I said, 'Just stay right there, I'm coming to get you and then you can follow me back here.'"

So Karl walked toward his car, an open-air vehicle. His friend Logan—knowing that Karl had consumed too much beer—urged him not to drive. "I said 'It's only, you know, not even a mile down the road. I'm not going that far. I'm not even getting on a main road.'" Then another friend, Wayne, got in the back seat and he was like, 'Yeah, man, let's go!' Then another guy that I had met that night got in the passenger side and Logan said, 'Well, if you are definitely going to go, at least buckle up; buckle your seat belt.' And I was like, 'Alright man, alright.' And then I took off."

It was 2:00 a.m. The darkness was near complete in the unlit park area, with only small reflectors to guide the way. It would be difficult to navigate if one was sober—which Karl was not. Court records would later show that the "eight or nine beers" he had consumed made his blood-alcohol level .14—far above the .08 legal limit.

"We made it out of the wooded area and we were on our way," he remembers. "Not long after that I was about to hit one of the reflectors on the side of the road. I veered to the left; I still saw the reflector and I overcompensated and veered to the right, and then overcompensated again to the left. When I over-compensated back to the left, my two right tires popped and my hubcap flew. Wayne was in the backseat holding on to the roll bar; he hadn't buckled up and he catapulted out of the vehicle. The car rolled with me and the other guy; we were buckled into our seat belts, which saved our lives. And I mean it all happened very, very quickly."

The high schoolers used a cell phone to call the police, and ambulances soon arrived on the scene. Karl's friend Wayne was airlifted to the nearby Carolinas Medical Center in Charlotte, North Carolina. At first, things got better for Wayne; there were signs that he would survive. Severely weakened from his crash injuries, however, he contracted pnuemonia in the hospital and things got much, much worse. Wayne succumbed to pneumonia and died nine days after the wreck. Karl was responsible for the death of his close friend.

Karl faced felony charges and time in prison. He didn't argue the charges. He pleaded guilty and was ordered to pay hospital, court, and funeral fees and perform supervised community service.

Today, Karl says: "My life changed drastically. What I do believe is that everybody makes his or her own life. For me, this is my life. I can't lie down and take the easy road out. Because if I do that, then Wayne's life meant nothing."

Karl reflects on the day that changed his life: "Teenagers are probably the most stubborn people in the world. You're not going to tell them anything, especially if they've got their mind set on doing something. There's nothing that my friends could have done to stop me driving that night. The only thing they could have done was physically take the keys from me."

Kaia's passion for performing was cut short the night before her first day of college.

KAIA PARKER

While Karl was the driver of the car that killed his friend, Kaia Parker was a passenger in the car that killed her. She was 19 when she was killed in a drunk-driving crash in August of 2000. Kaia had been a rebellious teen but she was in the process of turning her life around; the day after she died was to be her first day of college.

Both Kaia's and Wayne's stories point to a startling statistic: The National Institute on Alcohol Abuse and Alcoholism reports that half of those under 21 who die in alcohol-related crashes are passengers. Kaia's story exemplifies another statistic: The National Highway Traffic Safety Administration says that when it comes to fatal teen crashes, boys are far more likely to be at the wheel than girls. And males are twice as likely as females to drive under the influence of alcohol.

We spoke to Kaia's mom, Lee, who told us that at the time of Kaia's death, "I think her interest was in moving forward with her life and having a fuller range of experiences from any she had had up to that point. She did a lot of experimenting between the ages of 14 and 19, but I feel that she had turned a corner and she was leaving behind the wild woman that she had become."

While her mom admits that Kaia had a wild streak in her, she also received excellent grades and pursued an interest in dance—which she practiced five or six times a week.

In her senior year of high school, Kaia met her first serious boyfriend, Josh. Lee could see that Josh was far from perfect. "He had major anger tantrums," she says. "He had an attitude and was verbally abusive. And he was very, very possessive of her and very rude to me. Very argumentative. He was also very reckless. Extremely reckless." Kaia met Josh on Halloween of 1999 and they were together for nine months. Lee comments: "Because Kaia had never had a serious boyfriend before, I think it was a very important thing for her on some inner level to experience that sort of relationship. And she was willing to compromise her values to a very large degree for that to be the case."

Lee had many talks with Kaia about Josh that last summer of her life. In the days before Kaia was to head off to college, Lee witnessed a big change in the North Carolina teen's personality and outlook. She was clearly preparing herself for the next chapter of her life. One of the things she planned to do before leaving for college was break off her relationship with Josh. "And Josh knew it," Lee emphasizes. "He actually confided that to me later. She was done with the relationship; she was ready to move on. She was talking about wanting to major in French and business and had lots of plans."

Kaia went to see Josh the day before she was to head off to college. Lee shares what she knows of the meeting: "They were both drinking, and I believe that they were drinking Bloody Marys. I know that he had a .15 level alcohol and she had .11. It might have been somewhere around three in the morning; he doesn't remember anything. He has no memory . . . But I think he probably passed out at the wheel. They were heading back to my house and he missed a turn. He was speeding down a hill on one of the local roads going about 55 or 60 around a 25-mph zone. There was a sharp turn and he lost control and crashed into those two trees at the bottom of the hill. Josh, he doesn't remember anything that happened, so we'll never know the complete story."

What Lee does know is that she was awakened by the phone call that is every parent's nightmare. "The phone rang about five in the morning. It was the emergency room saying Kaia was there and they'd been working on her for an hour and they couldn't save her." Kaia died from massive internal injuries.

BRIAN CROUCH

Lenny Crouch, who lives in upstate New York, tells the story of his son, Brian, who was tragically killed in a car crash four years ago. Brian was 20 and Brian was intoxicated.

Lenny describes his son as being very quiet and very warm, with an infectious smile. When it came to alcohol use, his father said, "I would say he was a social drinker. Kids said he wasn't really, you know, a wild partier, but socially he would drink with them. But Brian and his friends always took cabs when they needed to. What was unbelievably ironic was that in the pocket of the pants he wore the night he died he had the card for the cab company that he had always used."

Brian (right) and a friend celebrate their high-school graduation.

Brian was a student at Sienna College in New York State. He was a marketing major and he had just completed his junior year. Lenny tells us that Brian, in the process of moving out of his dorm room to spend his summer in the family house, had dinner there, with the family, for the first time in a while. His mom made jambalaya, and Brian told them that he had plans that night. He "was going out with a girl who was a senior and was going to be graduating that week. He was going back up to campus because they had some activities for the seniors the week prior to graduation." Lenny made it clear: "If you're going back to campus you're not going to drink, you're not going to drive; you're not going to "do it."

Lenny explained to us: "So, he left the house that night, headed off in the car. All looked well as he went up the street." However, Lenny found out that at some point later Brian and some friends wound up at a bar just off the lower edge of the campus. Lenny describes it as "a hangout for the local college kids." It apparently was a bar that served minors or accepted their fake IDs.

"Ultimately what happened was he left the bar, at a time that was unknown. But at some point he left there in his car, driving the car by himself. It was maybe a mile from the bar to the campus up a hill on a kind of winding road. Because the road was the way to the dorms, it was a piece of highway that Brian had driven hundreds of times before."

The story has a tragic end. "Somewhere around one-thirty-ish, quarter-to-two in the morning, there was a banging on my door at home," Lenny recounted. "When I finally woke up and looked out one of the windows I saw two people, police officers, standing in front of my door. The police officers introduced themselves and one of them started to cry. I had trouble understanding the officer but she said what sounded like 'He's not coming back,' and I was like, 'What do you mean he's not coming back?' The officer said, 'He was in a crash by school, he went off the road, the car is in a ditch.' Well, my wife had woken and was behind the door and she just let out one of those really guttural screams. Then it truly hit me. My son was dead." Brian had died of fatal injuries.

These stories are painful but necessary reminders of things we don't want to know; reminders that traffic crashes are the number one killer of teens. Still, along with the incredible heartbreak of these stories, we have to believe that something important can be learned from each of them. Fatalities can occur no matter where you are seated in the car. Passengers—even sober passengers—are just as likely to be killed as drivers.

The life of every teen may very well depend on that teen's acute awareness that a car with a drunk driver behind the wheel is no longer simply a vehicle. It's a deadly weapon.

CHAPTER 5

THE TEEN MIND UNDER THE INFLUENCE

A CONVERSATION WITH DR. AARON WHITE

5 THE TEEN MIND UNDER THE INFLUENCE:
A CONVERSATION WITH DR. AARON WHITE

AARON WHITE IS AN ASSISTANT RESEARCH PROFESSOR AT THE
Duke University Medical Center in Durham, North Carolina. His specific
areas of interest and expertise are the effects of alcohol on brain
function—particularly learning and memory—and the relationship
between adolescent brain development and the risks of alcohol and
other drugs.

He speaks regularly to high school students and their families,
addressing the particular vulnerabilities that arise from changes
within the brain during the teen years. Dr. White is dedicated to
finding effective ways to facilitate communication between parents
and teens about substance abuse and other potentially risky behavior.

Q: **What is it about a teen's brain that is different from an adult brain?**

A. *There are many changes that occur in the brain during the teenage years that we didn't know about until recently. I think the changes in the brain really explain the tumultuous behaviors and emotions in the teenager. People used to say, "It's all hormones, their hormones are raging." It's true that there are changes in the hormone levels. However, it's not the changes in hormone levels that cause all the developments that we see in teenagers—it's changes in the brain.*

Q: **What is the biggest change that occurs in the teen brain?**

A. *The frontal lobes, located in the area behind the forehead, are being dramatically remodeled during the teen years. So, the teen years are not an extension of childhood. It's not like the teenage brain is just going linearly from being five to being 25 with you just fine-tuning the development of the brain. It's not like that at all. The teenage years are all about really shaping the frontal lobes, which end up determining who we are as people, how we view ourselves, what our goals are.*

Q: **What task do the frontal lobes perform?**

A: *The frontal lobes are what allow humans to do things that your dog can't. The frontal lobes let us think about the future, think about what we want to do in the future, and then make decisions to get us there. At the same time they control our impulses, to [help us] do the things that are consistent with those goals. So those frontal lobes allow us to basically engage in goal-directed behavior. For instance, most of us want to eat all the junk food that we can, whatever our preferred junk food is. But our frontal lobes tell us it's not consistent with our long-term goals, such as being healthy and fit. Our frontal lobes are constantly in a battle with the rest of our brain to try to keep us from doing things that are inconsistent with our long-term goals.*

Q: **Do you remember what it was like when you were a teenager? Can you relate your memories to your work today?**

A. *I remember coming into school on a Monday morning and thinking, how can I possibly get through this week? A week seemed like an eternity.*

It's because our sense of the future is totally different when we're 15. If you asked a 15-year-old what their plans are, they're not going to tell you about the decisions they've made for retirement. I never thought about retirement plans when I was 15. However, when I was 25 I was thinking about retirement plans, which were still 40 years down the road. The frontal lobes, which allow us to think about the future and make plans, are under dramatic construction during the teen years, so not surprisingly teens don't think as much about the long-term consequences of their behaviors. They're thinking about satisfying their immediate needs. It also puts teens at greater risk of doing something that's dangerous because it feeds that feeling of invincibility, because teenagers can't fully think through complete consequences of an action. So a teen has trouble saying "If I try to jump a wall on a skateboard and I break my leg then I'll have medical expenses, and 20 years down the road my leg's probably going to hurt when the weather changes."

Q: Do the frontal lobes develop simply through experience, or do they develop biologically as well?

A.   *I think it's primarily through experience. At about age 11 for females and 12 for males, it's like the switch gets thrown and all of a sudden the frontal lobes go into massive remodeling mode. The switch is probably thrown as a result of hormonal changes, but once it's thrown what you end up doing with it is guided by your experience. Parents of teens need to help guide them through the process with positive experience.*

Q: In your research, why are teenagers so much more apt to be risk takers than adults?

A.   *I think that we are inherently built to take risks and explore the world when we are adolescents. The critical part of the process of adolescent development is the transition from being a child—when we're dependent on caregivers—to being able to function on our own. I think the worst thing we can do is keep teenagers from taking risks, because they're not going to get through the challenges of adolescence. We just have to help guide them into taking healthier risks. Healthy risks are synonymous with real challenges. It's like playing a sport or anything where there's a possibility of failure. On the opposite end of the spectrum, getting drunk is a risk but there's no potential for growth there. So it's an empty risk.*

Q: What do you think some other examples of healthy risks are?

A. *Aside from athletics, activities such as joining a debate team or being part of a drama club are healthy risks. Those are real challenges in that if you can do them, if you succeed, you've built your confidence, you've shown that you're capable of doing difficult things. And that really facilitates the transition into adulthood. There's always a possibility you're going to fail miserably. But even if you do there's still natural growth there. On the other hand, getting drunk—you really can't fail at it. But what do you get if you succeed? You get nothing. So that's what I mean by "empty risks" verses "healthy risks" or "challenges."*

Q: How does alcohol affect the brain?

A: *What alcohol does in general is it knocks your frontal lobes out. It takes your frontal lobes out of the equation for a while. If you walk into a bar to get drunk, you might as well just hang your frontal lobes on a coat rack, because they're going to be inoperable. You are then far more likely to make an unsafe choice.*

Q: What's the difference between the effects of alcohol on teenagers as opposed to adults?

A. *For teens, the circuits in their frontal lobe are far more fragile. You don't have all the skill sets in place that you will once you're an adult. A teen is not as good at driving a car, not just because the teen brain is changing, but because they haven't had as much experience. So, if you add alcohol, it makes it extremely dangerous.*

In addition to that, there are clear differences in how alcohol affects the brain in a teenager versus an adult. There is evidence that in the teen brain, the parts of the brain that make memories are much more sensitive to alcohol than in the adult. There's a phenomenon called blackouts, where people wake up in the morning and they don't remember what they did. We used to think that blackouts were something that only happened to alcoholics, and that's totally wrong. I've done several studies looking at blackouts in younger people, like college students, and they're ridiculously common because the parts of the brain that make memories are more easily shut off when we're young.

Q: **What are the consequences of this?**

A. *I think that teenagers are more likely to do stupid stuff anyway, because of the way they're built. You add alcohol to that and now you're more likely to make destructive decisions. If you drink enough to the point where you're not making new memories, the risk is there for doing really stupid stuff and not remembering what you did.*

So the impact of alcohol on cognitive functions—like making new memories, decision-making, impulse control—I think those things are greatly impaired when teenagers drink, more so than in adults. Because you [as a teenager] are already built to take risks, you already have trouble controlling your impulses, and all of a sudden you add alcohol—that's not a good combination.

Q: **What other parts of the teen brain does alcohol impact?**

A: *We know, for instance, that when the brain is changing in the womb, alcohol wreaks havoc on that brain. So it makes sense that, given all the changes occurring in the teen brain, alcohol would probably wreak havoc on teen brain development. Basically, anytime the brain is developing, alcohol can mess that up. So far all the evidence is consistent with the hypothesis that alcohol disrupts the development of the teen brain.*

Additionally, I think alcohol impairs plasticity of the brain—it keeps your brain from changing with experience. That's what memory is all about. Memory is really a change in the brain with experience. Alcohol shuts down memory. It shuts down changes in the brain with experience. It does that more with teens. So I think both the short-term and long-term consequences are greater for teens.

There's a study at the University of California in San Diego that recruits kids from the community and looks at their IQs. The study starts when the kids are 13, then tracks them over the years. They track which kids drink heavily and which kids don't. What they find is that the kids who end up on the heavy-drinking trajectory score more poorly on IQ-type tests down the road relative to kids who don't drink. Even though they were all comparable at the beginning, the kids who go down the pathway that involves heavy alcohol use end up showing cognitive deficits relative to those who didn't drink heavily.

Q: What advice do you have for parents of teens?

A: I think parents should embrace the changes of teens rather than fight them. Help them discover all the healthy forms of risk-taking you can find so they can build confidence and explore the world in a relatively safe way. Also, it is important to talk to your teen about alcohol and drugs and other issues of health and safety. Be certain your teen knows how you feel about these issues. Communication between parents and kids really seems to diminish the odds that teens will abuse alcohol or drugs.

FOR MORE INFORMATION . . .

If you are interested in learning more about Aaron White's research, visit his web site, titled "Topics in Alcohol Research" at: **www.alcohol-info.com**

CHAPTER 6

ARRIVING ALIVE

AVOIDING DANGERS OF DISTRACTION & OTHER SAFE DRIVING IDEAS

ARRIVING ALIVE:
AVOIDING DANGERS OF DISTRACTION & OTHER SAFE DRIVING IDEAS

6

WHEN IT COMES TO DRIVING, ALL TEENS ARE BEGINNERS.

And therein lies a problem: Statistics show that crash rates for teens are several times greater than those of older, more experienced drivers. While making the documentary *Smashed: Toxic Tales of Teens and Alcohol,* we were saddened to discover that injuries from motor vehicle crashes are the leading cause of death and disability among teens.

Why all the crashes? According to the CDC's National Center for Injury Prevention and Control, teens are more likely than older drivers to underestimate the dangers in a hazardous situation. Moreover, teens have less experience coping with such situations. Just like an airline pilot, who must accumulate a number of tutored and then solo flight hours before becoming skilled enough to fly with passengers, teens need to clock time on the road to become experienced, safe drivers. Also, teens can be oblivious or careless about their inexperience, rebelling against the idea of "thoughtful driving."

At the NIH, Bruce Simons-Morton, Ed.D, chief of the Prevention Research Branch, looked into this risky business. His research team studied the behavior of both teens and adults on highways and on local roads, particularly in the immediate vicinity of high schools. They found that "both male and female teenage drivers drove faster than the general traffic." Also, teens tend to be tailgaters, allowing less space between their car and the vehicle ahead of them than experience demands. Add this to their faster-than-average driving speed and the combination is deadly, with or without alcohol.

Next we went to driving instructors around the country to see what guidance they give beginning drivers. Their safe driving tips for teens are simple, but they're not always obvious.

NO SAFETY IN NUMBERS

For those young drivers who have recently received their licenses—16- and 17-year-olds—the likelihood of a crash increases with each additional passenger in the car. It makes sense that the more passengers, the more distraction, which in turn means less focus on the road.

Cynthia Dulgov, an instructor at Mr. D's Driving School in Tucson, Arizona, advises that "teens should not have any other individuals in the car with them—at least for the first year—until they get more comfortable in their driving skills." She's talking about along-for-the-ride friends, of course, not parents. Parents are always strongly encouraged to accompany a teen driver. The more in-car supervision they can give the new driver in the family, the better. And safer.

ABOUT BOYS

You could call it gender-bias—if there wasn't research to back it up: The NIH study mentioned on page 74 also revealed that when a teen boy was driving with another teen boy, he was 150% more likely to drive 15 mph over the speed limit than he would be when driving alone. The NIH gave the lowest marks on driver safety to teenage boys accompanied by another teenage boy.

TIME AND SPACE

These next daunting observations, which are based on simple physics, come to us from Bruce Leininger, a former driving instructor for the Montgomery County, California, Sheriff's Department. He is now a driving instructor with the National Traffic Safety Institute. "For every 10 mph, you travel 15 feet per second," Leininger points out. "So, at 30 mph, you go 45 feet per second. At 70 mph, you're covering 105 feet per second."

Time it for yourself: *One thousand one. One thousand two. One thousand three.* At 70 mph, you've just driven the length of a football field in three seconds. Clearly, keeping a safe distance between cars—probably a far greater distance than a teen thinks is safe—is critical. From cell phones to backseat chatter to a quick glance at a map, a momentary distraction of even three seconds is enough to cause a crash. The American Automobile Association (AAA) Foundation for

Traffic Safety agrees that distraction is one of the biggest problems facing teen drivers. "Does answering a cell phone take longer than three seconds?" Leininger asks. "Does looking for a CD of your favorite band take three seconds?" That's why, in Leininger's world of safe driving, there are no cell phones and your CD changer is preloaded and installed in the trunk before hitting the road.

It boils down to this: On the road, we must constantly think about what could happen in the next three or 12 or 20 seconds. Tell your teens to: Scan the road. Look ahead. Learn to peer through the windshield of the car in front of them. If stuck behind a vision-blocking van or truck, put an extra measure of space between it and their own vehicle.

FATAL FOOD

Eating in the car can be catastrophic. As Bruce Leininger says, "What's the very next thing a kid wants to do once they're behind the wheel of a car? Eat." Anytime you're eating something, at least one hand is occupied and you're more apt to take your eyes off the road to take another bite. (And what about food that requires more than one hand? It takes two hands to eat a burger or slice of pizza). It's very clear that drinking and driving can kill; so can eating and driving.

CELLULAR DANGERS

Cell phones contribute to crashes in several ways: Aside from the distraction a phone conversation may cause, using a cell phone requires one hand, leaving a driver only one remaining hand for the steering wheel. One-handed steering can create an enormous handicap if there is a sudden change in traffic, if someone darts in front of you, or a pothole or road obstruction appears. Driving is not a multi-tasking sport. It needs 100 % attention and focus. This may be out of sync with the reality of contemporary life—and not just for teenagers.

Nonetheless, every safe-driving organization in the country—including the AAA Foundation—recommends putting cell phones away while driving. Yet shockingly, as of this writing, only New York State and the District of Columbia have outlawed driving while holding a cell phone. Even more shocking is the handful of states that have actually passed laws to specifically protect legal cell-phone use on the road, preventing towns within the state from limiting their use. As you can see, it really is up to you, the driver, to protect yourself.

THE 10 AND THE 2

Experts suggest the famous "10 and 2" or "10 minutes to 2 o'clock" position as the safest place to grip the steering wheel when driving. Here's how it works: Pretending the steering wheel is a clock, you place your left hand where the 10 would be, and place your right hand where the 2 would be. This position offers the greatest stability and control for drivers of all ages.

As for using a cell-phone headset while driving, there is no definitive research proving whether the practice is safe or unsafe. But it's hard to argue with the fact that the simple act of engaging in a conversation can pull a teen's attention off the road. So consider playing it safe and asking your teen to save his or her phone conversations for times when they are not driving.

While cell phones are clearly a driving distraction, a new and potentially even more dangerous diversion is about to become widely available. The entertainment industry is poised to offer shows direct to your cell phone. Soon, TV, movies, and elaborate video games will be options for all cell users.

Many parents were happy in the late 1990s when SUVs and minivans were introduced with on-board DVD and video-game players for backseat use. They were welcome babysitters—especially on long trips—for the tots seated in the rear. But now these tots are preteens getting ready to drive. If, for as long as you've remembered, you have always played games or watched movies on the road, will you be able to resist the temptation now that you're in the driver's seat and the entertainment is right on your cell phone? Even having a friend sitting in the front passenger seat who is watching a music video while you drive would be incredibly distracting. Since eyes taken off the road for only a split-second can contribute to a crash, the best advice is to keep show business out of the car and the cell phone safely put away.

BEWARE OF THE BAG

Air bags save hundreds of thousands of lives each year. But, as Leininger cautions, "many people don't have a healthy respect for the power of an airbag." Here's what he's talking about: If you carry a soda can or coffee cup in your hands while you're driving, you may also be taking your life into your hands. When struck by a deployed airbag, that container is probably going to fly straight toward your face at 200 mph, causing serious damage to your eyes, nose, teeth, or brain-protecting temple—your whole face is fair game. Leininger explains the phenomenon with a baseball analogy: "If a driver is holding a soda can, the soda can is the ball, the airbag is the batter, and the driver's face is the catcher!"

As a passenger, you have responsibilities, too: Avoid propping your legs up on the dashboard. It may look cool and it may be comfortable, but if the car stops short and the airbag deploys, your body can fold in half, your spine can break, and you can become a paraplegic for life. Manufacturers have slowed the impact of airbags in many newer vehicles: when a crash occurs at less than 25 mph, then the car's bag unfolds at the equivalent of 100 mph, instead of the regular 200 mph. That said, at 100 mph, airbags still have serious crush power and they can injure whatever body parts may get caught beneath them.

IT'S LIKE NIGHT AND DAY

Art Dulgov, a public school teacher and owner of Mr. D's Driving School in Tucson, observes that "teenagers tend to have accidents when they're driving at night." Often, teens are just learning their way around their communities; the lack of daylight can make things look unfamiliar. "Even if teens have grown up in the place in which they're driving, during daylight hours they can find a lot of things. But at night, the landscape becomes very, very different," he adds. As a result, teen drivers who think they know all the landmarks may have to search harder to find them. This searching draws eyes away from where they should be focused: the road.

Then there's the fact that darkness affects drivers at any age. "You know, there are [blinding] lights, especially oncoming headlights," says Dulgov. "The roads are more difficult to see, and it's harder to judge depth perception." An obstacle that you might easily avoid in daylight—a small animal, a fallen branch, or even a person—becomes a blind hazard. Parents, limiting your teenager's drive-time to daylight hours is a simple way of decreasing his or her odds of being in a car crash.

Dulgov offers this last piece of advice about nighttime driving: More people drive impaired by alcohol at night than they do during the day, so it's vital for teens who will be driving after sundown to hone their defensive driving skills. (After all, you never know when your teen may have to swerve to avoid an intoxicated driver.) Unfortunately, however, school-based driving instruction generally takes place during the day. Therefore, it's really important to sharpen your teen's nighttime driving skills by practicing with him or her in the evening, paying special attention to routes most often traveled.

ONE-STOP SHOPPING

Many states offer a learner's permit at age 15, meaning that by the ripe old age of 16, many kids are on the road solo. Driving instructors advise that not only should parents know exactly where these 16-going-on-17-year-old drivers are headed, they should also limit the permitted stops en route to just one.

For example, allow your teen to drive to the mall and back—not to the mall, then across town to the record store, and then across town again to a friend's house before coming back home. The greater the number of stops, the greater the number of chances that the teen will become distracted. If you explain the reasons for one-stop trips, your child just might understand and accept the rule.

HOT WHEELS

What types of cars are safest for teens? Certainly not sport utility vehicles. "SUVs, with their higher center of gravity, are not the safest. Their rollover fatality rate is much higher than that of a smaller vehicle," says Cynthia Dulgov. "Teenagers tend to forget what they've learned in driving school once they're on the road, where they may drive using risk-taking behavior. Then, whatever they run into, they're going to have even greater damage with an SUV. That means they could kill someone." Furthermore, large vehicles such as SUVs, vans, station wagons, and big luxury sedans can be very difficult for an inexperienced driver to maneuver.

CRASH-TEST DATA

Driving instructors encourage parents to remember that teens are twice as likely as adults to crash their cars. That means it's important to study crash-test data for whatever auto—or autos—your teen will be driving. Additional things to look for in a vehicle are multiple airbags, anti-lock brakes (which are enormously helpful to beginning drivers) and a solid "roll cage," which can save your child's life.

Compact vehicles, however, aren't safe either. Too often a teen, being the newest driver in the family, gets the family's smallest, lightest car to drive: the kind of car most vulnerable in a collision. Compact cars are generally too small to provide adequate protection from a collision—there simply isn't enough metal between the car's outside and the people inside. Plus, these diminutive cars collapse more easily upon impact, whether impact occurs during a collision or rollover crash.

Finally, driving instructors warn against cars that are "too cool." When it comes to buying a car for teens, especially boys, some parents veer toward a high-performance model with a "hot" engine. While a souped-up sports car may get mom and dad major brownie points in the short term, a performance car's powerful motor and racing-car reputation may encourage risky driving behavior. A less sexy, more sensible car—like a solid mid-size or full-size car— is a safer choice.

STATING THE OBVIOUS

According to the CDC, teens have the lowest rate of seat belt use. In 2001, 14% of high school students reported that they rarely or never wear seat belts as passengers. Furthermore, studies show that the worst teen drivers are the very ones who don't wear their seat belts. In 2002, the NHTSA reported that 77% of teens who die in crashes—regardless of where they were sitting in the car—were not wearing their seat belts. Nearly half of these deaths involve alcohol.

Remarkably, there are states that mandate seat belts only for front-seat passengers. If you live in one of these states you can blame your state representative. Or you can put blame aside and lobby to change your state's law.

SEAT BELT LAWS VARY BY STATE

According to the Insurance Institute for Highway Safety, as of this writing in 2005, 49 states require all front-seat passengers and drivers to wear a seat belt—New Hampshire is the only exception. However, only 18 states also require all rear-seat occupants (adults and children alike) to wear safety belts.

The remaining 32 states do not have rear-seat safety belt laws that apply to adults—although most of them do have laws that pertain to children under 16. These 32 states are: Alabama, Arizona, Arkansas, Colorado, Connecticut, Florida, Georgia, Hawaii, Illinois, Indiana, Iowa, Kansas, Louisiana, Maryland, Michigan, Minnesota, Mississippi, Missouri, Nebraska New Hampshire, New Jersey, North Carolina, North Dakota, Ohio, Oklahoma, Pennsylvania, South Carolina, South Dakota, Tennessee, Texas, Virginia, West Virginia, and Wisconsin.

To learn more about seat belt laws in individual states, visit: www.nhtsa.dot.gov/people/injury/airbags/ OccupantProtectionFacts/appendixc.htm

In the meantime, urge your teen to make his or her own seat-belt law by requiring all passengers to buckle up whether or not the law requires it. And parents, make sure you buckle up! Studies show that when parents wear seat belts, their children are more likely to wear seat belts, a simple habit that can save their lives down the road.

NOT "FINE TO DRIVE"

No teen can control everything that crosses his or her path, including other teen drivers who may act irresponsibly. But all teens can control 100% of their own alcohol and drug use, and they can choose the people they drive or ride with.

You need to stress to your teens that they don't ever have to get into a car with someone who has been drinking! Nor do they have to drive if they have had even the SMALLEST amount of alcohol! Both points are important to keep in mind, because there is a common misperception among drivers both young and old that having just a few drinks is nothing to make a big deal over; that you can consume a little alcohol and still be "fine to drive"; that a couple of beers won't impair driving skills or get you a DUI. That's a dangerous and potentially deadly belief. Research shows that drivers who've had even one or two drinks are more likely than nondrinkers to be involved in multiple-car collisions.

Why? Because reflexes slow down—way down—as alcohol enters the blood-stream. Because your ability to concentrate is compromised, and your peripheral vision is limited. Even the smallest nip of alcohol can impair the way you react, which in turn can increase the likelihood of crashing into another car. Common scenarios include not seeing—and then plowing into—a car that has pulled into the lane in front of you, made an emergency stop, turned suddenly, or run a red light. These scenarios do not ever have happy endings.

The smallest drink before driving is bad enough, but after more than five drinks your senses and skills are so impaired that the likelihood of being in a single-car crash—with your car doing the crashing—goes way, way up. Stationary objects like a parked vehicle, a tree, a fence, a guardrail, a wall, a building—or even a ditch, ravine, or body of water—are all just waiting out there for the next drunk driver to come along.

A WORD ABOUT DRUGS

Alcohol, of course, isn't the only substance that can impair driving: Drugs—whether illicit, prescription, or over-the-counter—can be extremely destructive as well. If you're a teen or a parent of a teen with a drug or substance abuse problem, or if you have questions on the subject, these web sites can provide an excellent starting point for you. However, if someone you know has been abusing drugs, please seek professional help immediately.

www.teens.drugabuse.gov
The world's largest resource for current information and materials concerning substance abuse and alcohol prevention, intervention, and treatment. This site is managed by the NIDA (National Institute on Drug Abuse, part of the US government's National Institutes of Health) specifically for teens. Parents can also visit **www.drugabuse.gov**, another NIDA site featuring helpful information, facts, links, and resources.

www.health.org
This site is a clearinghouse of all the information and documents written by the US Department of Health and Human Services and SAMHSA (Substance Abuse & Mental Health Services Administration). The web site addresses concerns of all age groups, and includes sections specifically for teens.

www.drugfree.org
The Partnership for a Drug-Free America is a nonprofit coalition of communication, health, medical, and educational professionals, working to reduce illicit drug use and help people live healthy, drug-free lives. Many parents and teens are familiar with the Partnership's television, radio, and print advertisements.

www.aacap.org
The web site of the American Academy of Child and Adolescent Psychiatry, a nonprofit organization, provides a good resource on teens and substance abuse. Its home page lists scores of articles on issues that every family faces.

WHY THE GRADUATED DRIVER'S LICENSE IS A GOOD IDEA

*"To learn some new tricks
Ooh, it takes such a long time."*
—from "A Human Body" by Roger Taylor, Queen

Driving isn't easy. It may take only a couple of months to conquer the basic skills of moving a car forward, but it can take years to feel comfortable under all driving conditions. Motor vehicle crashes are the leading cause of death for young people aged 15 to 20, causing about one-third of all fatalities in this age group. The National Highway Traffic Safety Administration reports that—taking into account the number of miles driven —teenagers are involved in three times as many fatal crashes as all other drivers put together. One of the leading causes of these teen crashes is simply driver inexperience.

In 1979, recognizing that teen drivers needed more time to develop their driving skills, Maryland became the first state to implement a Graduated Driver's License (GDL) program. California came next, in 1983. Each state set specific restrictions for specific stages in the process required

to earn a full driver's license. Before 1979, teens could often get a learner's permit sometime in their 15th year and a full license (aka "regular driver's license") about six months later.

The GDL is a system designed to phase in young beginners to full driving privileges as they mature and develop their driving skills. There are typically three phases to a full graduated system, requiring beginners to remain in each of the first two "restricted" stages for a specific minimum time period, before graduating to an unrestricted license, usually at age 18. During these early phases, young drivers hone their driving skills within the following confines: a restriction on nighttime driving, a restriction on the number of fellow teens allowed in the car, and a strict "zero tolerance" policy on drugs and alcohol use. Each state's requirements differ slightly.

States that have firmly adopted these policies generally see a 20% decrease in crash rates for teens— and many lives are saved. In addition, night-driving road safety results are usually better in states that require teens to gradually master nighttime driving with adult supervision, according to a study by the AAA Foundation for Driving Safety.

As of this writing, 45 states and the District of Columbia have enacted at least one key element of graduated driver-licensing. Unfortunately, while some states have implemented strong

programs, others have not. Though it's true that every state writes its own laws for driver's licenses, parents can—and must—determine for themselves what they believe is appropriate for their teen. In other words, living in a state without a GDL on the books doesn't mean that you can't establish the life-saving restrictions recommended by the GDL in your own household!

To learn which states support GDLs, you can visit: www.highwaysafety.org/safety_facts/qanda/gdl.htm

THE BOTTOM LINE

"You're going down the road nice and happy and everything's wonderful, and suddenly something starts to go wrong, and you have an impact," says Bruce Leininger, summarizing the devastation that driving distractions can cause. "And from that moment of something going wrong to the moment of impact, there's generally just three to six seconds. And in that brief time, that teen's family album is damaged forever." Remember: Count one thousand. Count two thousand. Count three thousand. That's how long disaster takes.

ADVICE TO PARENTS

Make a deal with your teen about drinking and driving. Make a realistic plan to help them avoid ANY involvement with alcohol and automobiles. It's one of the most valuable agreements parents can have. How?

Prearrange a time when your child is required to "check-in" with a call home. This can be a requirement of going out, regardless of whether your teen is at a party, the mall, a dance, or hanging out at a friend's home. This call allows parents to use their instincts in order to gauge their child's sobriety.

Discuss potential drinking-driving scenarios in advance—from being too tipsy to get behind the wheel to having difficulty finding a sober person to drive him or her home. Then create comfortable options like these, which are available to your teen.

NO MATTER WHAT:

- Regardless of the place or the time—even if your child knows it means waking someone up to come out in a thunderstorm and drive across town—he or she should know it's okay to call and should feel comfortable asking.

- Your teen has permission to stay at a friend's house, or to invite friends to stay at your house.

- Make it clear that you will pay for a cab without question, no matter how much it costs, if that's the safest, most viable ride home.

The important thing is to talk about these and other options in advance. Open, frank talk can prevent tragedy on the road. See Chapter 7 for options and scenarios you can discuss together.

WHAT WOULD YOU DO IF...

REHEARSING STRATEGIES TO AVERT TRAGEDY

7 WHAT WOULD YOU DO IF . . .
REHEARSING STRATEGIES TO AVERT TRAGEDY

"WHAT-IF" SCENARIOS ARE THE STUFF THAT MOVIES ARE MADE of—but they can also be homegrown dramas to help families prepare for tough situations. This chapter provides some what-if scenarios for common drinking-driving circumstances that most young people will face at one time or another—no matter who's behind the wheel. Abstaining from alcohol isn't the same thing as abstaining from danger—an astounding 30% of the kids in a recent national survey reported getting into a car with an intoxicated driver within the past month (National Youth Risk Behavior Surveillance). There would probably be another even more disturbing statistic if it was known how many kids *unknowingly* got into cars with intoxicated drivers!

We can't foresee every drinking-driving situation, but on the following pages we include some that the teens we talked to have encountered, whether these teens drink or not. Following each scenario are options—some lousy, some solidly safe. The time to explore these options together is right now, while your child still has choices instead of consequences.

THE FAMILY "CODE"

As Dr. Knight suggested in Chapter 2, one way to help your teen get safely out of uncomfortable situations is to have a family code word or phrase. That way, your teen can call and say "Did Anna leave a message for me?" or "I forgot to walk the dog." You'll know what he or she really means is, "I need you to give me a ride home," or "I'm worried about my ride home." Teens we've talked with agree that this works and saves them from embarrassment in front of their peers.

"WHAT-IF" SCENARIOS

Experts tell us that role-playing risky situations and dealing with internalized peer pressure can be enormously helpful in avoiding true-life disasters—negotiation, manipulation, and avoidance are realistic approaches for teens to use. As one teen we spoke with said: "I think it usually comes down to pride for most people . . . If you're the one drinking, you don't want to be taken out of control by having to have someone else drive your car, so the best solution for that person is kind of manipulating them to think that they're not being taken out of control. If you're a passenger . . . you don't want to appear to be a wimp or worry-wart—you may just tell yourself to shut up and everything will be fine. So safe ideas that make a teen look in control, decisive, and firm will keep them from feeling embarrassed to speak up—they can sound like they're being the smart leader of the group rather than the whiner." Other teens told us that if they are at a party with a friend who's too drunk to drive, they let them fall asleep—a better way to "crash."

These scenes will affect your teen far more powerfully if you play them out together, making each situation personal. Actors know that improvising is an invaluable tool, and this can be equally true in your own home. Where our script says "[name]," substitute the name of someone you know who just might be involved in such a sticky scene. Think of the first car your daughter is about to own; the party your son is headed for on Friday. If you are that son or daughter, turn the parents in our scenarios into the parents who will be waiting for you at home. Everyone in the family can create his or her own imaginary scenes; chances are they'll spark new insights for both parents and teens. To make this exercise as viable and realistic as possible, we presented these scenarios to a diverse group of teens across the United States. Their word-for-word responses are included, in case you get stuck and need some lines for your script. An important note: This is *not* a test. Be certain not to appoach it as one. Make sure your child knows nobody's grading his or her paper. There may easily be more than one good choice in each instance, or options you haven't considered—or that we didn't list. Use this exercise as an opportunity to discover potentially life-saving options—and what you can do to make these options a part of your lives.

SCENARIO #1: "IT'S JUST A FEW BLOCKS AWAY..."

It's Friday night. You're at a friend's house in the neighborhood, and someone arrives with a few six-packs of beer. Soon, it seems as if everyone has had a couple. Suddenly you all get hungry and a friend suggests going for pizza a few blocks away.

BAD IDEA:
- Drive there slowly.
- Drive somewhere closer.
- Walk to the pizza place. (Drunk pedestrians are an endangered species, too.)

SAFE IDEA:
- If you've had NOTHING to drink, suggest that you drive everyone to the pizza place—and back. ("I call driver! I'm the only sober one," or even "I really feel like driving. Okay?")
- Offer to go and get the pizza yourself. ("I don't mind running out. Want anything else while I'm out?")
- Order in. ("Let's just get it delivered. It would be so much easier," or "Let the delivery guy drive—none of us are in any shape to.")

SCENARIO #2: TO GET IN OR NOT TO GET IN

You're out for the evening. Someone you've seen around school and always wanted to hang out with offers you a ride home. On your way to his or her car, you realize that, although adorable, this person is not sober. You don't want to mess up the chance for a hot date, but you don't really want to risk a drunken drive, either.

BAD IDEA:
- Get in. (Neither of you will look so cute after a crash.)

SAFE IDEA:
- Make it clear how you feel about being asked—and how you feel about drinking and driving. Suggest you drive. ("Nice car, mind if I drive?")
- Both get a ride with someone else. ("I'm going to get a ride with [name], but I want to keep hanging out with you. Why don't you just come with us?")

SCENARIO #3: PARTY PROBLEM

You go to a party with a bunch of friends. When you arrive, there's a big crowd. You split up to mingle, agreeing to meet up later. A few hours later, you notice your ride is out on the back porch with a drink in hand.

BAD IDEA:

- Pretend you hadn't noticed.
- Think "how dangerous could a couple of drinks be?"
- Believe them when they say they're fine to drive.

SAFE IDEA:

- Find another safe ride. Check with the host for suggestions if you're stuck. ("Would you mind giving me a lift home? [Name] was supposed to, but he/she's in no shape to drive.") It's smart to look out for the others in your group, too. ("You guys should probably find another ride. Want to come too?")
- Call your parents for a lift, both for you and your friends. ("Mom/Dad, things didn't work out like I thought they would. We're kind of stuck here and want to leave. Can you come get us?") Or use your code phrase, if you've rehearsed.
- Ask someone else to call their parents. ("Can you call your parents to pick us up? I was going to go with [name], but she's been drinking. I know your parents are cooler about this kind of stuff than mine are.")
- Call a cab for you and your pals. (It'll be a lot cheaper to split the fare than pay for a hospital bill.)
- Call a friend who's elsewhere—or home—but sober.
- Just stay put. Ask if you can spend the night.

SCENARIO #4: THE DRINKING DATE

Your date is waiting outside the house for you and you're excited about the night ahead. You hop into the car and before long you realize your date—who usually doesn't drink—has already had a few drinks at a friend's house. You're headed for a party and you really want to go.

BAD IDEA:

- Listen to your date's insistence that he or she is fine and continue on your way.

SAFE IDEA:

- Suggest pulling over and switching seats. You'll keep the relationship alive. Literally. ("Look, if it's okay with you, can I drive? I've really been looking forward to this party, and I'd really rather spend time with you there than at the hospital.")
- If your date won't switch seats, ask him or her to pull over. Refuse to get back in the car unless you are allowed to drive.
- If your date won't pull over, the "I'm-about-to-vomit" ploy never misses (see page 32). Note: You don't need to be a girlfriend to try this effective tactic. Saying "I have to pee" works too.
- Call home and ask if you can bring the car back in the morning.

SCENARIO #5: THE FAMILY WHEELS

You've borrowed the family car to go out. By the end of the evening, you're at a friend's house, and you realize you're unable to safely drive home. It's after midnight, and you're terrified that you will never get the car again if anyone finds out.

BAD IDEA:

- Drive home as carefully as you can. (Imagine asking for the car again after you wreck it.)

SAFE IDEA:

- Give the wheel to someone who's sober. ("Can you drive my car home? I think I've had one too many, but I can't leave it here.")
- Have a friend call his or her home. ("Hey, can you call your parents? I'm too drunk to drive home, but my parents will kill me if they find out.")
- Call home and say you've made a mistake and need someone to come and get you. Making the responsible decision not to drive drunk, even after acting irresponsibly, is more likely to establish trust with your parents and increase the chance of getting that car again. ("Mom/Dad, can you come pick me up from this party? Sorry, but I messed up and I just don't feel like I should be driving home.")

SCENARIO #6: HOME ALONE

Your parents are out for the evening and you've invited a bunch of friends to your house. Someone brings a pizza, someone else brings some beer. (Or someone brings a pizza and heads for your parents' cabinets to look for alcohol. Which they find.) Your parents come home—earlier than they'd planned—and your friends want to hit the road.

BAD IDEA:
- Say goodnight and send your friends on their way.

SAFE IDEA:
- Invite them to stay over. ("My parents are cool. Why don't you guys just crash here?")
- Ask your parents to drive your friends home. ("Mom, Dad, I invited these guys over and I don't think they should drive themselves home. I know it's late, but would you mind taking them?")
- Call a sober friend to pick them up and take them home. ("Can you come over and give these guys a ride?"

SCENARIO #7: NEW WHEELS

Finally—you've got your own car! The big party is less than half a mile away, but you decide to drive anyway. By the end of the evening, however, you wish you hadn't.

BAD IDEA:
- Drive home, letting your ego tell you that you are the best captain of your ship.

SAFE IDEA:
- Ask a friend who's sober to drive your new wheels. You'll be taking much better care of your new car—not to mention yourself—if you do. ("It would suck if I messed up my car the first day I had it. Want to take it for a spin and drive me home? You can stay over.")
- If no one takes you up on that, leave your new wheels safely parked right where they are. ("I don't think I can handle driving right now. Can you drop me off when you're ready to leave?")

SCENARIO #8: BACKSEAT PARTY

You're driving with some friends. You're on the way to a sporting event when someone in the backseat pulls out a beer and passes it around.

BAD IDEA:
- Since you're the driver, and you're not sipping that beer, don't worry about it.

SAFE IDEA:
- Ask them to put the bottles or cans away. Stop and throw them in a garbage can if the containers are open. ("My car, my rules. And I say no alcohol. It's not cool. We can get pulled over and then we're all in trouble.") (In most states, it is illegal to drive with any open alcohol in a vehicle. Under the 1998 Transportation Equity Act for the 21st Century, a program was established to encourage states to adopt what's known as "Open Container Laws," which forbid the possession and consumption of alcohol in passenger areas.)

SCENARIO #9: PUT YOURSELF IN THE DRIVER'S SEAT

You're hanging out with a buddy who claims to be sober but obviously isn't. Your friend is adamant about being fine to drive, which may have been true at the start of the evening but certainly isn't now. You don't want to accuse him or her of lying, nor do you want to start an argument. But you know you should be the one behind the wheel.

BAD IDEA:
- Let him or her convince you they are sober enough to drive. (You may actually meet people who sincerely believe—particularly after a couple of drinks—that they drive better after drinking.)
- Avoid an unpleasant scene and pray.

SAFE IDEA:
- Don't let him or her convince you. Tell your friend you hope he or she would do the same for you. ("You are obviously not okay to drive, and you should know how stupid it is for you to do this right now. Do you want to get us both killed? Let me be your chauffeur. You can return the favor some other time.")

- Suggest you both ride with someone else so it doesn't seem as if you're trying to be cooler than your friend—even though, as it happens in this instance, you *are* cooler. ("Look, let's just both go with [name]. Then everybody's happy.")

SCENARIO #10: WHICH WAY DID THEY GO?

You go to a party thinking you have a ride home. There's been a significant amount of alcohol at the event, which ends unexpectedly. Your ride is nowhere to be found—but you want to leave the premises ASAP.

BAD IDEA:
- Hitch a ride with whomever's going your way, not knowing their condition.
- Walk home.

SAFE IDEA:
- Stay put until you can be sure you've got a safe ride.
- Call home. ("My ride just disappeared and I'm not sure about some of these other kids. I thought I had everything covered for tonight, but it's not working out that way. Help!")
- Call a friend who's elsewhere—or home—but sober.

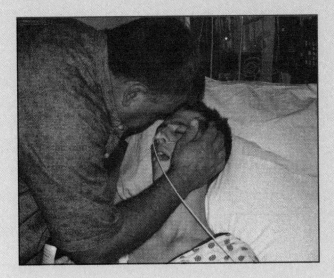

SMASHED:

TOXIC TALES OF TEENS AND ALCOHOL

ABOUT THE DOCUMENTARY

A VIEWING GUIDE

ABOUT THE DOCUMENTARY
SMASHED: TOXIC TALES OF TEENS AND ALCOHOL

Smashed: Toxic Tales of Teens and Alcohol, the documentary, takes a hard, sobering look at the devastation of teenage drunk driving. Filmed inside University of Maryland's Shock Trauma Hospital in Baltimore and aboard Maryland's fleet of EMS helicopters over many months of special access, it follows six kids who survived to tell their stories of broken bodies and shattered dreams.

From the phone call every parent dreads ("We believe we may have your child") through the desolating drama of recovery for those fortunate enough to survive, *Smashed* takes aim at the often-overlooked issue of teen drinking and driving by authenticating how tragic the typical teenager's illusion of invincibility can be.

Smashed was created as a cautionary tale for teen drivers and passengers alike. Whether it's driving with a quart of vodka or "just a few beers" on board—or just accepting a ride with a cute guy who's consumed them—the film does not preach. Rather, it opts for brutal honesty by graphically revealing the near-fatal accidents that can turn an adolescent into a helpless infant.

The unvarnished stories in *Smashed* are about drivers and passengers; males and females in diverse situations. But they all entered Shock Trauma because someone made a bad decision. Each of the teens and their families consented to be a part of the documentary with the hope that by participating, they might help prevent yet another tragedy.

Tracy never imagined she'd suffer a traumatic brain injury when she went with her partying pals to a diner to satisfy the late-night munchies. Timmy, at the tender age of 15, drank a case of beer and rode off into the sunset on his ATV, hitting a tree head-on when he swerved to miss a rabbit that darted into his path. Warren was the handsome, "most outgoing" senior in his class according to his yearbook. He had no idea that accepting a ride from a friend who'd drank a few beers would render him impulsive, aggressive, and depressed —resulting from the brain trauma he suffered—and eventually would lead him to spend some time under house arrest. And Katie, who took a ride from "a guy who was hot," had to give up her college career. She can't even follow a movie because her memory is so bad that she can't keep track of a plot.

All these individuals share the trauma of ambulances, ICUs, operating rooms, physical therapy, and messed-up lives. The worst of it is the fact that their trauma could have been prevented.

Smashed: Toxic Tales of Teens and Alcohol was produced and directed by Karen Goodman and Kirk Simon (authors of this book), an award-winning wife and husband team whose previous documentaries have earned three Academy Award nominations, several Emmys, and a duPont-Columbia Silver Baton. The film was honored with a Prism Award (the Entertainment Industries Council Award for outstanding accomplishments in the accurate depiction of alcohol and other substance abuse), and the Parents' Choice Award. *Smashed: Toxic Tales of Teens and Alcohol* was produced for HBO, where it was originally broadcast. Please note that *Smashed* is not intended for young children.

Nothing in the film is re-created. Unfortunately, it's all too real.

A VIEWING GUIDE

TALKING WITH YOUR TEEN AFTER VIEWING SMASHED

Initiating a conversation about drinking and driving can be an uncomfortable proposition for the parent of a teenager. That's where *Smashed: Toxic Tales of Teens and Alcohol* comes in. But the discussion after viewing Smashed mustn't be the only talk on the subject that you have with your teen.

Smashed can provide the impetus for a series of conversations that continue to the point where your teen actually expects you to bring up the subject of alcohol and driving. Yogi Berra once said "It's déjà vu all over again," and that's how your teen should feel about the frequency of talks concerning drinking and driving. Anything can revive the personal reality and the urgency of the subject, whether it be a mention on a TV show, an article in the newspaper, or the sight of an erratic driver on the road.

Just watching *Smashed* with your teen is only half the journey—this book can help take you the rest of the way. Arrange to stay in the room with your teen after the DVD is over so you can both talk about your reactions. We all know teens are edgy, and they are liable to race out before you can get two words out, so you need to plan ahead. Try this: Before you watch the DVD together, make it clear that it's not over when it's over. For instance, just say—without letting it sound like a school assignment—"After we've watched the DVD, let's stick around and talk about it, so you can tell us what you think." The strength of this film is that it's real: Real kids in real-life situations. Nothing staged, nothing reenacted. When teens watch the DVD with their parents—and that's the way to see it for the first time—it's vital that they discuss their reactions while the power of that reality is disturbingly fresh.

To help spark the conversation, here are some preliminary questions and activities. Don't feel bound by a need to stick to these specific suggestions; what's important is to have an ongoing, open, and honest conversation with your teen about the consequences of drinking and driving. You can also start additional discussions by referring back to *Smashed* when you see an article about a drunk driver in the newspaper or on television in the weeks after viewing. Remember, whatever works for your family is the right thing to do if it keeps that conversation alive.

QUESTIONS FOR TEENS

- How do you feel after watching *Smashed: Toxic Tales of Teens and Alcohol*?

- In the documentary, Warren says "I never thought it would happen to me, not in a million years." Do you feel this way?

- In the film, Timmy's dad says, "Everybody thinks they're invincible—nothing can happen to me—and you just make that one dumb mistake and then that's it, your life changes forever." Do you agree with this statement? Have you ever done anything involving alcohol that you've regretted? Have you ever put yourself in a situation that you now believe is unsafe?

- At the end of the film, Timmy is revisited at his birthday party. In his interview he says that he doesn't think it's wrong to party—if you know your limits. Do you agree with Tim? What would you say if you could speak with him?

- Do you think young people take drinking and driving seriously enough? Is it easy or difficult to keep the consequences of drinking and driving in mind? Why?

- Do you have friends who drink and drive? Have you had conversations with them about it?

- Katie got in the car with "a boy who was hot." She didn't know this young man—nor did she know "he'd had a few beers," as her brother later told her. Would you get in a car in a similar circumstance? How can you distinguish a safe ride from an unsafe one? Why are so many passengers victims of drunk-driving crashes, even if they're sober?

- Do you think your life can change in an instant because of a bad decision?

- Does the family have a stated policy about underage drinking?

- If you were in an unsafe situation and weren't comfortable with your options for getting home, what would you do? Would you call home? Why or why not?

FURTHER ACTIVITIES AFTER VIEWING THE DOCUMENTARY

- List all of the excuses you have heard or can think of why someone would choose to drive after drinking. Can you think of a good response to each excuse?

- List all the incidents you have heard of, or seen, where teens have been physically hurt after drinking alcohol and driving.

- Have you ever made a destructive decision involving alcohol and driving? Make a list of responsible alternative decisions you could have made.

- From your group of friends, make a list of people you know who you think make destructive decisions. Try to describe what makes these people act this way.

- From your group of friends, make a list of people you know who you think make responsible decisions. Try to describe what makes these people act this way.

- Have you ever felt you were the victim of peer pressure? Did you give in to the pressure? Can you describe circumstances where you would stand up for your beliefs?

SKILLS TEENS NEED TO ADDRESS ALCOHOL-RELATED ISSUES

Julia Taylor is an educator and guidance counselor for the American School Counselor Association. She develops lesson plans to help teach high school students what she describes as "safety and survival skills." With a grant from the National Highway Traffic Safety Administration, Julia helped develop a *Smashed: Toxic Tales of Teens and Alcohol* lesson plan for use in schools and by community groups. When dealing with alcohol-related issues, she finds that high-school students need to develop what she calls six "Competencies." Since teenagers are risk-takers and historically have a "that will never happen to me" attitude, these Competencies help teens develop skills to lead them down safer paths. Following each Competency below, we've added a clarifying quote from an interview with Taylor:

- **DEMONSTRATE THE ABILITY TO ASSERT BOUNDARIES, RIGHTS, AND PERSONAL PRIVACY**
  "Teens are under extraordinary amounts of pressure to belong to a group. They also are surrounded by a culture where connectability is easier than ever. Through technology teens can reach friends, parents, the Internet, with the push of a button. This makes it more difficult to create personal space or say no."

- **DIFFERENTIATE BETWEEN SITUATIONS REQUIRING PEER SUPPORT AND SITUATIONS REQUIRING ADULT OR PROFESSIONAL HELP**
  "Teens are on an emotional roller coaster from the moment puberty hits and are often confused about their feelings. When teens are in trouble, they will generally go to their peers first. The first few lines of those conversations begin with 'Don't tell anyone I told you this' or 'if you tell anyone I will never talk to you again.' Teens are very loyal to friends and feel like they are betraying them if they report serious issues. However, I have seen a number of lives potentially saved this school year due to other students showing concern. In the long run, things work out for the best.

  Teens are also very comfortable sharing their feelings all over the Internet. Blogs, IMs, and e-mails are given to me daily as a school counselor. Teens need to know that if they feel something is really wrong, it probably is. Many times teens simply need to vent, and sometimes they need serious adult intervention. This directly correlates with the next Competency: to identify resource people in the school and community and know how to seek their help."

- **IDENTIFY RESOURCE PEOPLE IN YOUR SCHOOL AND COMMUNITY AND KNOW HOW TO SEEK THEIR HELP WHEN NEEDED**
  "Every teen should know at least two adults whom they can go to for help besides their parents. These people could include, but are not limited to, a school counselor, teacher, principal, pastor, family friend or relative, coach, or a friend's parent. They should also have hotline numbers handy where they know their call will be anonymous in case they get into a situation where they feel they could not possibly tell anyone."

- **APPLY EFFECTIVE PROBLEM-SOLVING AND DECISION-MAKING SKILLS TO FORM SAFE AND HEALTHY CHOICES**
  "Teaching teens to problem-solve is easy, teaching them to actually apply problem-solving skills is another story. Most teens have no idea what they really want to do, but they know what their friends want them to do. Teens need to learn how to think independently with these skills: state the problem, brainstorm a solution, assess the results, and know what to do if the first approach does not work. Teens live for the present moment and sometimes have a genuine inability to see the difference between right and wrong. Positive role modeling, especially at home, is an utmost necessity for teenagers to learn what their best interest is."

- **LEARN ABOUT THE EMOTIONAL AND PHYSICAL DANGERS OF ALCOHOL AND SUBSTANCE USE AND ABUSE**
  "Unfortunately, some teenagers are merely told that drugs and alcohol are 'bad' and not to use them. As *Smashed: Toxic Tales of Teens and Alcohol* demonstrates, there are many other physical consequences related to substance use and abuse. Moreover, the emotional consequences are endless and could include risky sex, date rape, depression, suicide, family problems, anxiety, lower grades, personality changes (to the point teens think they need alcohol to be themselves), peer rejection, and addiction."

- **LEARN HOW TO COPE WITH PEER PRESSURE**
  "The days of 'if you don't drink this beer you can't hang out with us' are generally over. The peer pressure teens feel is internalized, meaning they

feel they should have a drink (or two, or three, or four) to relax and fit in. Teens rely on friends to validate their thoughts and feelings. To feel good about themselves, they need repeated peer approval. Resilient teens cherish their uniqueness and have a good time being themselves. Role-playing risky situations and dealing with internalized peer-related pressure could minimize harmful effects. In addition, the fine arts of negotiation, manipulation, and avoidance are realistic avenues that are easier for teens to use. These all are directly correlated with how teens are raised and praised at home."

ESSENTIAL THOUGHTS TO REMEMBER

Parents should learn to make every discussion about drinking and driving a true exchange and not a lecture. Ask open-ended questions and listen to the answers without interrupting your teen. Set the mood so that your teen can talk about anything without a fear of judgment. Do this and future talks will be a lot easier.

Sometimes your teen will say something that upsets you. If this happens, it's vital to control your emotions. Getting upset or creating tension won't help. As David Crosby sings, "Just look at them and sigh and know they love you." If you express your feelings in a positive way, and react to things your teen may say in a positive manner as well, you'll surely achieve a better exchange.

What is perhaps most important is to be very clear about your expectations and to communicate your own values. Different families have different values and set a wide range of limits upon their children. If teens know that their parents have strong feelings about drinking and driving—and the parents serve as positive role models as well—they are less likely to put themselves at risk.

In our interview with Taylor, we asked her what central element to emphasize during parent/teen discussions. She stressed how important it is "to talk to teenagers about a plan, should they find themselves in a potentially dangerous situation. Teens who don't have a plan in place will drink and, instead of phoning their parents for help, they will put themselves and others at risk."

"Seeing is believing," and we believe that *Smashed: Toxic Tales of Teens and Alcohol,* along with this book, shows and says things that are desparately important for your teens to see and hear.

RESOURCES: Organizations

- **NATIONAL HIGHWAY TRAFFIC SAFETY ADMINISTRATION** (NHTSA)
  www.nhtsa.dot.gov
  A government agency dedicated to reducing vehicle-related crashes.

- **NATIONAL COMMISSION AGAINST DRUNK DRIVING** (NCADD)
  www.3dmonth.org
  A government agency that serves as an independent and unifying force among public and private sectors in order to advance effective solutions to the drunk-driving problem.

- **INSURANCE INSTITUTE FOR HIGHWAY SAFETY** (IIHS)
  www.hwysafety.org
  Publishes studies the organization conducted about various highway issues, including alcohol-influenced accidents.

- **MOTHERS AGAINST DRUNK DRIVING** (MADD)
  www.madd.org
  A nonprofit, grass-roots organization with the mission to stop drunk driving, support the victims of this violent crime, and prevent underage drinking.

- **RECORDING ARTISTS, ACTORS & ATHLETES AGAINST DRUNK DRIVING** (RADD)
  www.radd.org
  An international nonprofit organization that uses celebrity power to create positive attitudes about road safety.

- **STUDENTS AGAINST DESTRUCTIVE DECISIONS** (SADD)
  www.sadd.org
  A peer leadership organization attempting to provide students with the best prevention and intervention tools possible to deal with the issues of underage drinking, drug use, impaired driving, and other destructive decisions.

- **NOT MY KID, INC.**
  www.notmykid.org
  A group geared toward parents dedicated to raising awareness about youth and adolescent mental and behavioral health issues.

- **LEADERSHIP TO KEEP CHILDREN ALCOHOL-FREE**
  www.alcoholfreechildren.org
  An initiative to prevent the use of alcohol by children ages 9–15.

- **THE NATIONAL COMMISSION AGAINST DRUNK DRIVING** (NCADD):
  YOUTH RESOURCE CENTER
  www.ncadd.com/youth_reso_center.cfm
  The Center is designed to assist individuals, organizations, and others who are interested in reducing underage drinking.

- **ADVOCATES FOR HIGHWAY AND AUTO SAFETY** (AHAS)
  www.saferoads.org
  An alliance of consumer, health, and safety groups, as well as insurance companies working together to make the roads safer.

- **DRUNK DRIVING REFORM INITIATIVE** (DDRI)
  www.ddreform.org
  The purpose of this initiative is to bring together various reform issues and ideas in order to contribute to reducing the number of alcohol and other drug-related highway deaths and injuries, especially by repeat offenders.

- **PARTNERSHIP FOR A DRUG-FREE AMERICA**
  www.drugfree.org
  A nonprofit coalition of communication, health, medical, and educational professionals working to reduce illicit drug use and help people live healthy, drug-free lives.

RESOURCES: Online resources

NATIONAL INSTITUTE ON ALCOHOL ABUSE AND ALCOHOLISM (NIAAA):
- **College Drinking, Changing the Culture**
  www.collegedrinkingprevention.com
  A web site dealing with the problems of drinking in college, with separate solutions geared toward the variety of groups involved.

- **Make a Difference: Talk to Your Child about Alcohol**
  www.niaaa.nih.gov/publications/children.pdf
  A booklet for parents on how to address the subject of alcohol with their child.

NATIONAL HIGHWAY TRAFFIC SAFETY ADMINISTRATION (NHTSA):

- **A Guide to Safe and Sober Event Planning**
  www.nhtsa.dot.gov/people/injury/alcohol/PartiesRock/section1-3.html
  A guide to planning fun, alcohol-free events and parties.

- **Zero Tolerance Activity ideas**
  www.nhtsa.dot.gov/people/injury/alcohol/zero/page1/idea.html
  Activity ideas to promote zero tolerance in a community.

- **Promoting Zero Tolerance**
  www.nhtsa.dot.gov/people/outreach/safesobr/15qp/web/idpromo.html
  Information on the campaign for zero tolerance laws.

THE MARIN INSTITUTE:

- **Alcohol and Teenagers**
  www.marininstitute.org/Youth
  Focuses on ways for youths and adults to deal with the alcohol problems surrounding youths and adolescents, presented by an organization dedicated to reducing alcohol problems through environmental prevention.

SUBSTANCE ABUSE AND MENTAL HEALTH SERVICES ADMIN. (SAMHSA):

- **Talk to Your Child about Alcohol**
  www.family.samhsa.gov/talk/TalkAlcohol.aspx
  A resource for parents on how to talk to their child about drinking.

INDEX

SMASHED

Toxic Tales of Teens and Alcohol

The documentary *Smashed: Toxic Tales of Teens and Alcohol* was filmed inside University of Maryland's Shock Trauma Hospital in Baltimore and aboard Maryland's fleet of EMS helicopters. *Smashed* follows six kids who survived devastating alcohol-related crashes. It explores in heartbreaking detail the sudden devastation that drinking and driving can bring—and shows how difficult the road to recovery can be for those lucky enough to survive.

- Timmy, 15, after drinking a case of beer, drove his all-terrain vehicle into a tree when he swerved to avoid a rabbit.
- Andy, 19, was driving home after drinking a "few beers" when his open-air vehicle, going 70 mph in a 35-mph zone, hit an embankment and rolled over four times.
- Traci, 18, after a night of partying, went looking for late-night snacks with a drunk driver who crashed into a tree.
- Tom, 17, after sharing nearly a gallon of vodka with two friends at a local mall, fell off an escalator—and onto a stone floor 20 feet below.
- Katie, 16, got into a car with a "hot" guy, not realizing that he had been drinking. She ended up in a coma for over seven weeks and suffered broken bones and multiple internal injuries, and permanent memory loss.
- Warren, 17, got a lift home from a friend who had been drinking "a couple" of beers; the friend's car crashed, and Warren suffered brain trauma.

PRINCIPAL PRODUCTON CREDITS

Produced & Directed by KAREN GOODMAN and KIRK SIMON

Co-Producer & Editor NANCY BAKER

Cinematography BUDDY SQUIRES, KAREN GOODMAN, and KIRK SIMON
Filmed on Location at Shock Trauma Hospital, Baltimore, Maryland

Original Music DAVID GROVER
"Everything is Broken," Written and performed by Bob Dylan. Courtesy of Columbia Records By Arrangement with Sony Music Licensing

FOR HBO FAMILY:

Supervising Producer DOLORES MORRIS

Executive Producer SHEILA NEVINS

A PRODUCTION OF SIMON & GOODMAN PICTURE COMPANY for HBO Family